Praise

'The authors bring a stellar combination of
world-renowned experience in marrying two fields –
financial planning and emotional intelligence – that
creates an abundance of practical, science-based
information that will greatly benefit wealth
managers and their clients. The world is now
realising that incorporating knowledge and skills
related to emotion and emotional intelligence makes
a powerful and vital difference to a professional's
performance and results in high-stakes contexts.
This book has captured and outlined how emotions
need to be understood, respected and regulated, not
ignored and suppressed. *The Heart of Finance* will
help frontline financial advisers to read, understand
and influence the emotions of their clients to build
rapport and trust throughout the client journey
towards win-win investment decisions. The book
also offers practical tips and techniques that will
help advisers recognise and manage their own
emotions and wellbeing when things get tough.
I highly recommend this book to anyone working in
consultative, advisory or sales roles.'
— **David Matsumoto** PhD, Professor,
  San Francisco State University, and
  President, Humintell LLC

'*The Heart of Finance* is a highly relevant book for financial planners, particularly in today's world, where increasing value is placed on our client relationships. James and Cliff demonstrate the growing importance of emotional intelligence alongside good technical skills and provide real-life examples and case studies. Whether you are new to the advice profession or have worked in it for many years, this book will teach you something.'
— **Carla Brown** CFP, FPFS, TEP, Founder, Oakmere Wealth Management, and President, The Personal Finance Society

'This book does what it says on the tin: it gets to the heart of the role of a financial planner, using the science of emotional intelligence to offer practical suggestions in a financial planning context. For years, we've focused on building expert knowledge, which is of course important; this book offers human connection as an equal partner in the planner's skill set. That's hugely important for client outcomes and inspiring the next generation of world-class financial planners.'
— **Helen Longland**, Financial Services Learning and Development Director

THE
HEART
OF
FINANCE

Emotional intelligence for financial planners

James Woodfall and Cliff Lansley, PhD

Rethink

First published in Great Britain in 2024
by Rethink Press (www.rethinkpress.com)

Contents

Introduction   1

1 **Hearts, Minds And Money**   9
  What is emotional intelligence?   11
  Emotions   14
  Moods, traits and disorders   20
  Empathy   22
  EI quadrants and abilities   24
  Job performance   27
  Summary   29

2 **The Client Journey**   31
  Mindset and biases   33
  Communication styles   38
  Emotions, triggers and purposes   43
  How emotions affect decisions   46
  Research examples   50

Rapport and trust   51

A climate for information gathering   52

Skill builder   54

Summary   55

3 Preparing For Action   **57**

Check your tubes   59

It's not all about me?   60

You never get a second chance to make
a first impression   61

On the steps – mindset and focus   65

Skill builder   67

Summary   68

4 Initial Meeting   **69**

Engaging the client   72

Rapport building   74

FORCED model for rapport   76

Testing rapport   78

Deeper conversations – The Trusted
Adviser Method™   79

Sadness   84

Refractory period   86

Contracting   87

Surprise   88

Skill builder   91

Summary   91

5 Planning Meeting   **93**

Fact finding   94

Goals   97

Happiness   99

Risk   100

Fear   103

Prioritise   107

Skill builder   109

Summary   110

6 Implementation Meeting   **111**

Recommendations   112

Cognitive load   114

Vulnerability   116

More on ethics and dark traits   118

Closing the sale   121

Leakage   122

Contracting   124

Skill builder   126

Summary   127

7 Difficult Conversations   **129**

Let's start with you   130

Understanding your emotions   131

Anger   133

Disgust   134

Contempt   135

Managing your chimp   136

Seek first to understand, and then to be
understood   138

Dealing with death and other bad news   149

Sorry for my poor apology   151

Skill builder   154

Summary   154

8 Ongoing Service Work   **157**

Relationship management   158

Delivering value   160

Intermittent rewards   162

Personalised communication strategies   164

The social smile   166

Keeping relationships on track   167

Client referrals and testimonials   169

Skill builder   171

Summary   174

Conclusion   **177**

Notes   **179**

**Appendix: The Trusted Adviser
Method Questionnaire**   **185**

    Set 1: Establishing basics   186

    Set 2: Exploring financial behaviours
    and attitudes   187

    Set 3: Deepening understanding of
    values and future planning   189

Acknowledgements   **191**

The Authors   **193**

    James Woodfall   193

    Cliff Lansley   194

Introduction

T hose working in the financial planning profession have traditionally performed an intermediating role, acting as agents for clients, but times are changing, and clients' needs are changing too.

Nearly all advisers globally must meet strict regulatory standards and are required to hold benchmark qualifications. Technical training ensures that advisers are knowledgeable and can be trusted by clients to provide expert advice. However, clients aren't interested in qualifications; they expect you to be technically competent, and many are likely to be financially literate themselves.

Instead, they want you to understand them, to reassure them when needed, to motivate them to act, to listen to them and counsel them if appropriate – and there is currently no mandatory training for these skills. As a financial adviser, you play an essential role in the critical moments in your clients' lives, moments like marriage, death, divorce, loss of employment, retirement, starting a business, selling a business or moving home, among others.

What training do you have to deal with a client who is suffering from the grief of a lost loved one?

How do you invite clients to tell you what's really on their minds?

Can you recognise the subtle signs a client might be vulnerable and not understand your advice?

What do you do when a client is panicking and about to act against their best interests while in the grip of a fierce emotion?

Situations like these are the reality of your role. Financial planners across the globe deal with the emotions that come with their clients' life events every day. The difference between success and failure lies in the adviser's ability to respond in the right way, enhancing and growing relationships rather than damaging them. The combination of skills needed to do that in a high-stakes professional environment is called emotional intelligence (EI).

In this book, we will explore the skills and abilities which make up emotional intelligence. This will provide you with a competitive edge in a world where such skills are rare. In the job performance literature, IQ ranks highly in predicting performance, but you all have the IQ needed to pass technical exams, so it's your ability to build relationships with your colleagues and clients, manage the stresses of your role, and be an effective communicator that makes all the difference. These are emotional intelligence abilities.

What separates emotional intelligence from IQ is that, regardless of where you are today, you can increase your emotional intelligence score with training.

This book combines our experience in emotional intelligence, financial services, business and life to help you increase your emotional intelligence capabilities. James Woodfall is the author of *Financial Planning for Entrepreneurs*. James spent fifteen years as a financial planner and ran his own financial planning firm for half of that time, which was sold due to ill health at the end of 2022. James holds a Master's of Science in Communication, Behaviour and Credibility Analysis. As part of the fulfilment of that programme, James' dissertation research investigated the role of emotional intelligence in predicting performance in financial advisers. Today, James runs Raise Your EI, a training and consulting firm focused on providing high-quality, science-based training in emotional intelligence to help firms and advisers in financial services achieve success.

Cliff Lansley is the author of *Getting to the Truth: A practical, scientific approach to behaviour analysis for professionals*. He is an expert in training and development, having built and sold DPG Plc after twenty-eight successful years, and in 2008 founded the Emotional Intelligence Academy. Cliff is also a scientific adviser on emotional intelligence and behaviour analysis for WarnerBrosDiscovery, on their true-crime series *Faking It*, launched in 2017 and now in its seventh series. In 2020, Cliff completed a PhD, and his research focused on developing the new EmotionIntell model of emotional intelligence. As part of the PhD, Cliff secured a majority, global agreement from forty-three global experts who study emotion on a clear definition of emotional intelligence and its 'ability' components.

We met while James was studying for his MSc. James' study revealed that emotional intelligence significantly predicted job performance across various domains. However, these were not the only benefits uncovered in his research. Emotional intelligence is linked with increased happiness, higher professional status, better subjective health, improved quality of relationships, and more experience of pleasant emotions. While researching the relationship between the performance of financial advisers and emotional intelligence, we found that advisers with high EI achieve higher sales, obtain more referrals and retain more clients. Combined with the evidence that emotional intelligence can be taught as a set of abilities, and those who receive training show increases in many of the domains mentioned here, the lightbulb moment struck – this is how financial advisers should be trained, and that training will lead to improved performance.

What amazed us was that we could find no global training programmes teaching the applied science of emotional intelligence for financial services professionals. So, it seemed that, by way of opportunity, we could combine our expertise and create a leading training programme that financial services professionals could access, increasing sales performance, referral numbers, and client retention. This book contains the science and application of the training programme we created.

Regardless of how successful you are today, you could be leaving opportunities on the table. Even if you score high on emotional intelligence, there is always room for improvement. Our aim with this book is for the material within to become the foundation for communication-skills training for global advisers to sit alongside technical exams. This is important, as artificial intelligence is changing the advice landscape. At the moment, 'robo-advice' is not at a stage where your clients feel comfortable using it over the human interaction you provide. But that day is coming, so your focus needs to be on developing your skillset to achieve the best human interactions possible.

That is why we have written this book: to deliver the specific training you need in order to succeed in the modern world, and to future-proof your role. The tools and skills within these pages will help you develop new ways of working with your clients to deliver an outstanding human experience alongside the advice you give. The more you do that, the more business your clients will do with you, the more they will recommend you to friends, family and colleagues, and the longer they will stay working with you.

We also understand that advisers who invest in training and development act more ethically and navigate conflicts of interest better. We are passionate about the excellent work that financial advisers do for their clients, yet the level of trust in the profession needs to reflect this. It may be the work of a few harmful agents that has eroded some trust in the profession, but with the tools and concepts in this book, we are optimistic that, as our message is shared, behaviours will start to change, and the level of trust will increase.

This book combines the science and application of emotional intelligence and is written by authors with the expertise to deliver the knowledge you need for success. We will lay the foundations in the early chapters, and then the book follows a 'typical' client journey to help you understand where the skills can be applied. You'll be familiar with the stages:

- Preparation for client meetings
- Initial meeting
- Planning meeting
- Implementation meeting
- Ongoing service

We will also cover the difficult conversations you may need to have with your clients as you deliver your service, such as those that may come with life events or challenges. We don't shy away from complex topics, as we understand that you don't have a choice about what your clients bring to your meetings, but we will give you the skills so you can observe, react, and respond appropriately.

By the time you finish reading this book, you will know how to develop your emotional intelligence capabilities to improve your relationships and to leverage every day the benefits of increased income, referrals and retention. However, reading isn't enough, so we will also challenge you throughout to think about how you will apply the learning to change what you do to achieve the results you deserve.

ONE
Hearts, Minds And Money

Since the 1990s, American Express have run a year-long emotional intelligence training programme which aims to develop the emotional competencies of their financial advisers. These competencies include self-awareness, self-management, empathy, communication, difficult conversations and stress management. In the pilot for this project, participants attended a workshop teaching these emotional competencies. They began the programme by completing surveys to measure their EI and their overall wellbeing. The results of the pilot were staggering. There was a 46% increase in sales performance. Stress levels decreased by 29%. Positive states increased 24%. Trait anger decreased 13%. Quality of life increased 10%, and physical vitality increased 9%. Dealing with anger constructively and managing stress, for example, helped the participants meet the demands of their role, leading to these overall health and wellbeing outcomes. This translated into improved job performance.[1]

As a financial adviser, you deal with the hopes and dreams of your clients and their families, their life savings or the business they have run all of their lives. You are therefore dealing with people's hearts and minds.

As their financial adviser, you will usually get to know what scares or excites them. These emotions aren't always vocalised, especially by people who are more private, therefore seeing or hearing the subtle signs from their body language, their face or their voice can give you a huge advantage. Knowing how to read emotions and showing you understand your client will mean you can develop trust and rapport more easily. This will enable you to engage them in the financial planning process because they will notice that you know what is important to them.

Of course, this is not just about the client. Being a financial adviser is a demanding role. Therefore, it is important to manage your own personal challenges and stress. Understanding more about EI will help you do this, and what's more, this will translate into superior performance.

In this chapter, we will outline and define the key terms we will use throughout this book. We will define EI and show how it matters more than IQ or technical skills as a financial adviser. We will also give you the research evidence to support these claims. We will finish by giving you a chance to reflect on your own emotional intelligence abilities by taking an online test to prioritise and develop areas you might want to improve.

What is emotional intelligence?

Emotional intelligence is defined as the ability to perceive, understand and influence our own and others' emotions across a range of contexts to guide our current thinking and actions to help us to achieve our goals.[2]

The table below explains this in more detail.

The elements of EI

	Awareness	Understanding	Influence
Self	Our own physiological sensations and thoughts	Our triggers, impulses, reactions, potential impact on FA role	Managing our own emotions and reactions
Context	Consider time and place for client meetings/ interactions	Impact on success of the FA process	Select and modify to suit the client and your goals
Other	Read the room – what can you notice about client behaviour?	What are they saying? Are they thinking/feeling something else?	Manage the relationship constructively

© Emotional Intelligence Academy Ltd (2024)

The elements of EI, shown at the top of the four rows, are **awareness**, **understanding** and **influence**. These can then be applied to the aspects on the left – **self**, **context** and **other**.

Self

Let's consider each aspect, starting with **self**. If you can have an **awareness** of your own physiological sensations and thoughts as you deal with clients, this can help you check yourself if you are becoming angry at something the client has said, or over-excited about one of your own recommendations. Your client will pick up on your emotions and this will reflect in how they respond to you. Therefore, awareness of self is a bedrock of EI.

Let's look at the self in terms of the next key element of EI, which is **understanding**. Here, it is important to understand what has triggered your emotion. It could be another person, something they say or do, or a place or a thing that evokes a particular memory or thought for you. If you feel that your emotions impact your conversation with a client, then note what has triggered that response in you. Once you have understood those triggers, you can then bring in another element of EI, which is **influencing**, or regulating, that emotion before it contaminates or biases your decision making.

Context

When we have that awareness, understanding and influence over ourselves, we can then begin to monitor the **context** in which we are working.

In this case, you need an **awareness** of the context – that is, primarily, the time and place of client meetings. Will the client be more comfortable in their own home or business, or would they prefer to see how professional and established you are and want to meet you at your office? Or is a neutral place better, where there will be no power dynamics at play between you?

You can then aim to **understand** how the context can impact the success of the financial adviser's process. For example, is your client comfortable using the phone, Zoom or Teams? How will this impact the success of the process you will take them through? With this awareness and understanding, you can then **influence** the context by modifying it to suit your client's needs and your goals.

Other

Finally, you need to focus on the **other**, that is, the client. This depends on you having **awareness** of who the decision maker is, eg is it an individual, a couple, a company board, or another group? Is it somebody who's not in the room? Is the person you are meeting representing the real decision maker? Having this awareness can help you to **understand** what is going on for them. That is because the words they use will be, at one level, only the tip of the iceberg. You may not see what is going on beneath the surface, so you need to be curious. What are they thinking? What are they feeling? What do you notice about their behaviour? What do you notice about their words? Can you work out what's going on below the surface for them? If you are curious enough, you can discover all kinds of information that will help you provide a much better financial-planning experience for your client. Once you understand this, it will give you a chance to explore and clarify, so that you don't waste time and effort developing and researching a solution that's not right for them.

Then, on an ongoing basis, you can **influence** the relationship constructively by monitoring how the client or clients feel about you and the service you are offering throughout the process.

Emotions

When we deal with financial-planning clients, we deal with their wants, needs, hopes and fears. Because you are dealing with their hearts and minds, it is crucial to work out what they are feeling and thinking about you and the advice you are offering.

Emotions help us to deal with matters of importance to our welfare or the welfare of those we care about without thought, and there are some important things you should bear in mind about them:

- They are quick – often passing in seconds, or minutes at most. Some people think they are emotional all day, but that is not the case. Emotions have a smooth onset, a short duration, and a smooth offset, which together last around four to six seconds. If we keep getting re-triggered with happy moments or happy memories, then we will have a series of happy emotions and it will feel like we are happy all day. Some emotions, such as sadness, can be more enduring, whereas fear and anger are usually quite quick. Surprise is a little different as it only lasts a second or two and usually transitions into another emotion once we have worked out what is going on.

- They are orchestrated by the chemicals and electrical signals we have within our bodies which generate impulses we can often see and hear – we will come to this later.

- They are unbidden, which means they happen to us. We don't suddenly decide to be angry, for example. Anger happens to us when something interferes with our goals, and it happens in about 400 milliseconds without us knowing or having an awareness of this.

- They can be self-initiated. You can make yourself happy or angry by thinking about topics that can trigger that emotion.

- They can be constructive or destructive. They are all helpful if we learn to understand them and use them in our interactions and conversations. But they can also block collaboration. If a client experiences emotions that support the process of your work together, then they are constructive. If they get in the way, though, they can be destructive to the process and to the advice you're offering.

Emotions motivate behaviour that can save or enrich our lives. In your role as a financial adviser, they can help you build relationships. They can also get you into trouble if they are allowed to take over. Because of the power and speed of the onset of an emotion, you need to know when to stop and ask yourself if an emotion is appropriate for where you are now. As a financial adviser, you need to judge the client's and your own emotions and ask yourself if they reveal problems that are blocking rapport with the client and preventing their trust in you. If you believe they are having an impact, you may be better off pulling back to allow some time until you have both worked out what is getting in the way.

Core emotions

There are many emotions, although scientists tend to agree on seven core emotions that we may experience:[3]

1. Fear

2. Anger

3. Sadness

4. Happiness

5. Disgust

6. Contempt

7. Surprise

These emotions occur within half a second of something triggering them. Therefore, the resulting impulse linked to each of these emotions sets off its own orchestrated array of physiological changes throughout our bodies. These changes are designed to help us deal with these triggers. Some examples of these physiological changes include:

- Changes in heart rate, which can speed up or slow down

- Blood pressure changes

- Breathing rate changes

- Voice changes in volume, pitch and tone

- Changes to local blood circulation and the temperature of the body, eg when we feel fear, blood goes to the large muscles in the legs to prepare us to run

- Cheeks flushing with embarrassment or anger

- Increased eye movements, eye closure, blinking and changes in pupil size

The combination of these psychophysiological changes, expressed through the face and the body, can give you some useful insights into what might be going on for your client.

Facial expressions, even short twitches (called micro facial expressions), may appear when your client is trying to hide an emotion. Information which the client may want to hide but which may be helpful to your conversation can leak out subconsciously through their expressions due to key facial muscles being hardwired to the midbrain by the seventh cranial nerve. Consequently, reading those facial expressions, and connecting them to an emotion and a trigger, can be useful in understanding what's going on for your client.

This is not just about your client's emotions, however. You need to tune into your own body, too, to pinpoint your emotions before your client notices so that you can manage and influence your own reactions. If you feel tense, and your arms are folded, your fists or jaw are clenched, then ask yourself what is going on for you at that moment. What has triggered that emotion in you? What do you need to do to manage it?

If you feel frustrated, contemptuous or judgemental about your client, it will leak. It's difficult to control these strong feelings or your physiological responses to them. Therefore, being aware of how your emotions cause your client to react can give you an opportunity to switch your approach. Some people may start to feel contemptuous toward a client who doesn't seem to have done any thinking about how to manage their assets. This judgement can easily be reframed to respect and admiration towards them for coming to you for advice. If you feel contemptuous, that judgement will show in your body language, your voice and, usually, a little one-sided curl of your lip.

Remember that there is a difference between a reaction and a response, too. A reaction happens subconsciously, like the expressions on our faces and voice and body changes. A response is what we *choose* to do, and that choice comes once all the facts have gone through the thinking part of our brains, which is four times slower than the speed at which we experience an emotion.[4] No matter how much meditating you do, you won't be able to interrupt the impulses.

Moods, traits and disorders

It is helpful to differentiate emotions from other states such as **moods**, **traits** and **disorders**.

Moods are longer than emotions and often less intense, and we often don't know what has triggered them. Taking anger as an example, you might say that your anger feels ten out of ten, but an angry mood might be two out of ten. You could just be a little irritable.

You could wake up any morning in an irritable mood, but if you are in that state, how helpful will that be going into a client meeting? Later, we will show you how to manage your moods and regulate your emotions, which are skills that can be constructive or destructive depending on how effectively they are applied to the matter at hand.

Traits are the characteristics of a person – sometimes referred to as their **personality**. For example, you might say that someone who is often angry is a hostile person. It's a word that describes their personality and is often true about that person over time. Some scientists think that traits such as being hostile, shy or timid, for example, are with us throughout our lives, but others disagree and say that we can modify these traits.[5]

Traits characterise you. If you are a hostile person and generally dissatisfied with the world around you, this can put you in a perpetually irritable mood and that will prime you to become angry more readily, which can, in turn, put you into an irritable mood again. Being aware of this cause-and-effect relationship will help you personally, and in your relationships with your clients.

Disorders (such as a phobia or chronic impulsivity) can sometimes be destructive as they can distort reality and often need clinical intervention to prevent them from dominating the way we feel about the world and our lives.

This is important information for financial advisers. If a client seems fearful or apprehensive about a particular group of products you are describing (eg stocks and shares), they may have developed that 'phobia' from a previous bad experience. They may even have a more general anxiety disorder around risk which affects their reaction to the information you are giving them. Although you are not a clinician and it is not up to you to diagnose your client, being aware that some people have histories or attitudes that affect their emotions can be handy when you want to understand why things are getting a little heated between you and your client. Imagine that you have arranged to meet a client at your home and you discover they are allergic to cats, with your cat lurking on the back of the sofa they are sitting on. Or what if your client is claustrophobic but you meet them in your tiny office? This is why being curious about your client and understanding their emotions, triggers, moods and traits will help in building that trusting relationship you need as their financial adviser.

Moods, traits and disorders

Emotion	Mood	Trait	Disorder
Anger	Irritable	Hostile	Chronic impulsivity, violent
Fear	Apprehensive	Shy, timid	Anxiety, panic, phobia
Sadness	Blue	Melancholic, pessimistic	Depression
Happiness	Euphoric, contented	Optimistic	Mania, risk taking

© Emotional Intelligence Academy Ltd (2024)

Empathy

Having empathy means putting yourself in the shoes of another individual and understanding what is going on for them emotionally. This is a selfless act, and you have to give all of your attention to the person to do it. Empathy is key for a financial adviser. As your understanding of what your client is thinking and feeling increases, it will help you to deepen your conversation and your relationship, and this will develop trust.

There are three levels of empathy:

1. **Cognitive empathy** – 'I know what you're feeling though I don't necessarily feel it myself.' This level relies on recognising what others are feeling. This doesn't mean that you are going to be helpful or compassionate. For example, a poker player or a torturer might have this type of empathy.

2. **Emotional empathy** – 'I feel what you are feeling.' If a client talks about a loved one or an illness or death, then they may get into a sad state. If you have emotional empathy, you feel what the other person feels and you can therefore show that you understand. This will help you connect. If you are naturally an empathetic person, you will care and engage with your client easily. Be aware, though, that your client doesn't want you crying with them for hours – they want your advice, and you need to be skilled enough to know when to move to level 3.

3. **Compassionate empathy** – 'OK, I know you're feeling sad. I feel what you feel and I want to help you and deal with the situation that's creating this emotion you're feeling.' Here, we experience and apply compassion for our client.

Whether it is sadness, happiness or anger a client is experiencing, a good financial adviser will have the skills and confidence to advance through each of these levels appropriately so that they can help their client in a sensitive and caring way. They will be careful not to move to sympathy and feel pity for their clients because they know this can be condescending and judgemental, and they may appear detached and aloof to the client.

Our advice is always to connect and understand, but not to judge.

Also, watch out for emotional contagion. This happens when you pick up the emotion of your client from their voice or their face. If you master EI, you will be able to use this information about their emotional state while managing your own emotions to prevent it from contaminating you. You will be able to show the client you understand them but move the conversation on to a place where you can begin to help them through their emotion and give them the financial advice they need.

EI quadrants and abilities

Let's now dive deeper into what makes up EI. The *EmotionIntell* model is based on recent research which shows that most scientists agree that EI falls into four quadrants:[6]

- **Self-awareness** – recognising and labelling emotions as they arise in your body

- **Self-management** – interrupting and managing your reactions where they are inappropriate and instead responding to suit the goals required

- **Social awareness** – reading the behaviour of others so that you can fully understand what they are thinking and feeling

- **Social interaction** – building rapport and trust by interacting and influencing your client towards their goals

Within each of the four quadrants, there are three abilities, or competencies. These break down the quadrants, and we will build these twelve abilities with you in this book as you enhance your service to clients.

Then, at the end of this chapter, you will be invited to assess yourself against this model so that you can find where you are strongest and where you might need to develop. Don't worry, we will cover any development gaps throughout this book.

Job performance

EI matters more than IQ or general intelligence when it comes to performance in human interactions.[7]

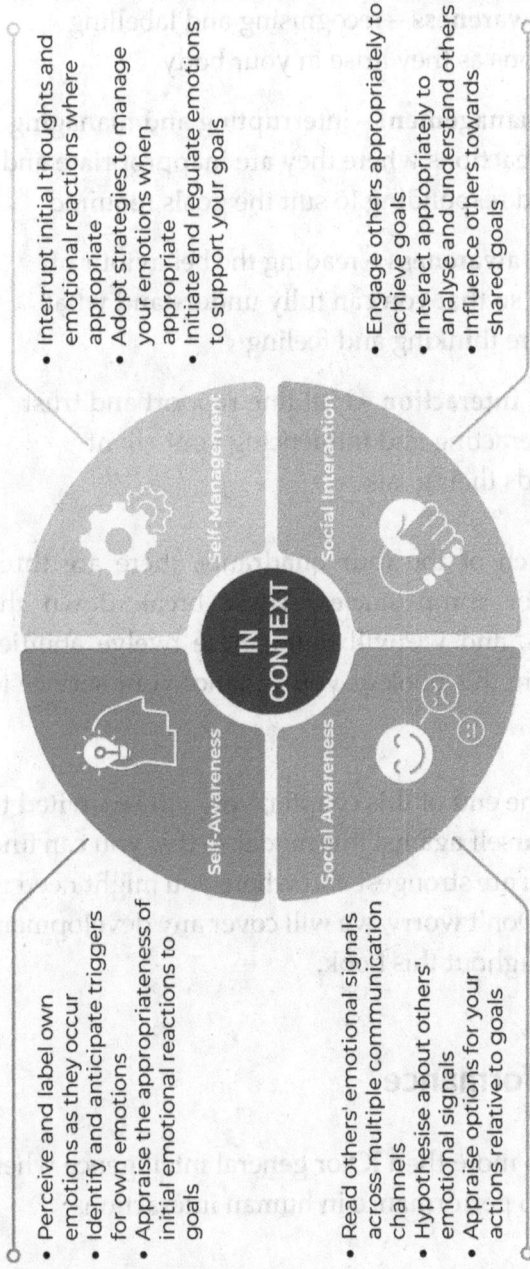

IN CONTEXT

Self-Awareness
- Perceive and label own emotions as they occur
- Identify and anticipate triggers for own emotions
- Appraise the appropriateness of initial emotional reactions to goals

Self-Management
- Interrupt initial thoughts and emotional reactions where appropriate
- Adopt strategies to manage your emotions when appropriate
- Initiate and regulate emotions to support your goals

Social Awareness
- Read others' emotional signals across multiple communication channels
- Hypothesise about others' emotional signals
- Appraise options for your actions relative to goals

Social Interaction
- Engage others appropriately to achieve goals
- Interact appropriately to analyse and understand others
- Influence others towards shared goals

© Emotional Intelligence Academy Ltd (2024)

Don't forget, a financial adviser needs to be qualified to operate, and those qualifications will have tested your knowledge and understanding within the discipline, which is more a scholastic quality.

IQ and technical skills don't matter as much as emotional intelligence when it comes to performance, although they are essential for carrying out professional roles such as that of the financial adviser, teaching or sales for example.[8] Consequently, if we can improve your EI and add that to the technical skills you already have, you will have both qualities, and that's the purpose of this book, because EI is vital in relationship building, in relationship maintenance, in sales and in conflict resolution.

These will be familiar to you as a financial adviser on each part of your journey with a client. Whether that is your first meeting with them, a subsequent meeting as you collect data and build up suitable products, when you finally close the deal and get their agreement on the best way forward, or, finally, when you pick up any issues later, such as environmental/market changes that impact their investment or if something changes in their family or their business.

Handling conflicts, fears and worries is at the core of being a financial adviser. Of employers, 71% value emotional intelligence over IQ when they search for new talent.[9] This is across all occupations and professions. EI has therefore become a new filter in recruitment selection because technical skills can easily be taught or will already be possessed by candidates. But if someone excels in technical skills but can't deal with people, isn't emotionally aware or cannot manage their own or other people's emotions, they will not perform as well as those with emotional intelligence.

Working as a financial adviser means you are responsible for the advice you give your clients, and this brings its own stresses. Therefore, EI helps you look after yourself, too.

Research into the relationship between EI and job performance has found that EI is an important predictor of performance.[10] The role of the financial planner is highly complex and cognitively demanding, and research has shown that advisers who are high in EI effectively manage the demands of their role better.[11] Managing your own emotions in difficult conversations, like those around mortality or illness, has been suggested in research to be important for selling life insurance.[12] Advisers who are high in self-awareness are able to label and manage any discomfort they have around the topic of death or illness.

These research examples reveal that EI is positively correlated with higher life satisfaction and self-esteem, and lower levels of insecurity and depression. It is negatively correlated with poor health choices and behaviour. Those who are low in EI are often less healthy and have problematic behaviour.

EI is also related to higher sales performance, increased referral numbers and greater client retention.[13] We showed at the beginning of this chapter the benefits of EI training on the performance of financial advisers at American Express. According to author and researcher Daniel Goleman, EI needs to be developed for it to translate into job performance.[14] While EI has been correlated with a number of performance outcomes, the greater increases come from developing your EI abilities, just like the advisers at American Express. As you read this book, think about how you will apply the knowledge to develop your skillset.

Now we'd like you to take stock of your own EI abilities with a short self-assessment. It will take you about fifteen minutes to complete. Following this, you can list your personal development areas so you can focus on the appropriate sections of this book to help you improve your emotional intelligence. You can access the self-report test here: www.eiagroup.com/ HeartOfFinance.

Summary

As a financial adviser, you deal with clients' hopes, dreams, life savings and businesses, engaging deeply with their emotions. You need to understand what excites or scares them so that you build trust and rapport. This will encourage them to participate in the financial-planning process, as they feel understood and valued.

Developing EI is key to this. In this chapter, we have defined EI and its importance to your role as a financial adviser.

We also discussed the characteristics of emotions and how understanding and managing them is essential for maintaining effective relationships with your clients.

We covered the three levels of empathy: cognitive, emotional and compassionate empathy. Developing these skills helps you to build trust and effectively support your clients.

Finally, the chapter discusses EI's four quadrants – self-awareness, self-management, social awareness and social interaction – highlighting its importance in performance, relationship building and handling stress.

TWO
The Client Journey

M arcus hates theme parks. When he was a boy, his father took him and his siblings when-ever they were away on holiday. You'd think, as a child, Marcus would have loved that. The prob-lem was that Marcus' father had a particular belief that meant Marcus' enjoyment of theme parks was forever ruined: his father believed that you should never waste money. He was going to get maximum value from the entrance fee no matter what it cost his family. He would march Marcus and his siblings into the theme park as soon as the gates opened, pay the entrance fee and then insist they got on every ride two or three times during the day. He'd only allow them to leave when the park closed for the night. As a result, he and his siblings ended the day, tired, hungry and hating the place.

Now, Marcus realises that he, too, has inherited this belief of not wanting to waste money. Recently, he bought a bean-to-cup coffee machine. It took him six months to part with the cash to buy it. For no other reason than he felt it might be a waste of money.

When he eventually bought one, he added the beans, plugged it in and turned it on... and had the best cup of coffee he'd had in years, leaving his wife to ask, 'Why have we been drinking crappy instant coffee for so long when we could have been having this every morning?'

Like Marcus, many of us may have emotions that are triggered by events or people in our past without understanding where they come from. Those emotional triggers can affect your success as a financial adviser if you don't reverse engineer them and manage such biases. That's why this chapter is so important. Here, we will cover the impact of emotional triggers on your client's decision making and emotions, mindset, biases, rapport and trust. We will also provide EI tips and techniques that will help you succeed throughout the general stages of preparation – initial meeting, planning meeting, implementation and ongoing service work. These stages are illustrated in the figure below.

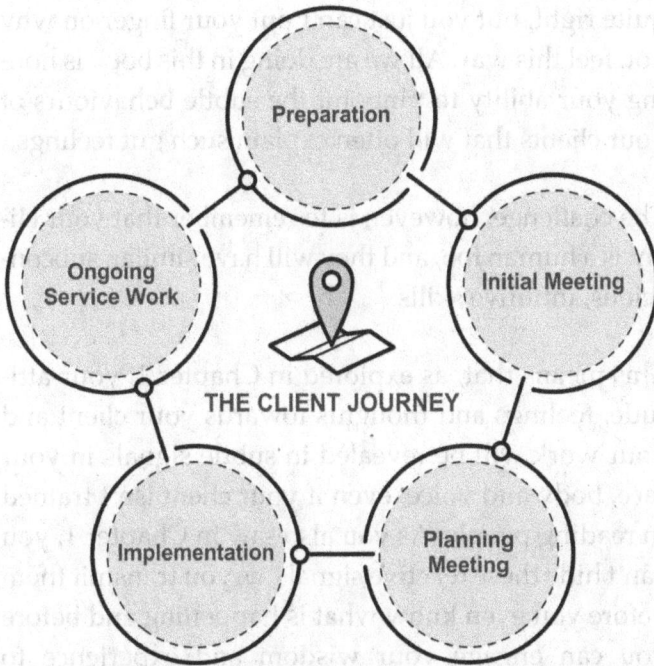

Preparation

Ongoing Service Work

Initial Meeting

THE CLIENT JOURNEY

Implementation

Planning Meeting

© Emotional Intelligence Academy Ltd (2024)

We have structured this book around this typical client journey and show you where EI can be applied throughout this process, which can have a huge impact on your success with your clients. Let's first look at mindset and biases before we start this journey.

Mindset and biases

Humans have evolved the ability to pick up on signals that don't fit. You can call this intuition or gut feeling – those times when you sense something is not quite right, but you just can't put your finger on why you feel this way. All we are doing in this book is honing your ability to pinpoint the subtle behaviours of your clients that will often explain such gut feelings.

The challenge, however, is to remember that your client is a human too, and they will have similar, subconscious, intuitive skills.

This means that, as explored in Chapter 1, your attitude, feelings and thoughts towards your client and your work will be revealed in subtle signals in your face, body and voice, even if your client isn't trained in reading people. As you also saw in Chapter 1, you can't hide these reactive signals, as you transmit them before you even know what is happening and before you can engage your wisdom and experience to interrupt your true thoughts and feelings (when they are inappropriate), and choose to respond differently.

You might, for example, judge a client to be inept, rude or unethical. Their behaviour may make you feel disgusted, contemptuous or angry. Of course, as a professional financial adviser, you will either put on a brave face and put your feelings to one side, attempt to regulate your emotions, and do your best for the client... or choose not to work with them.

But there is another way.

Instead of going into a session harbouring judgements and destructive emotions, you could instead adopt a mindset of curiosity. Go into the meeting accepting that the other person may have traits and habits that come from their past experiences, and try to understand what makes them the individual they are. This needs your total attention on the other person, but it can prevent you from moving into judgement and leaking your feelings to them – and the bonus is that giving someone 100% of your attention is the best compliment you can pay them, and they will notice it.

This can help you manage any conscious and unconscious biases, too. Biases such as:

- **Me Theory** – thinking 'If I was them, I would do this and that, etc'. They are not you, and your personal solutions may not work for them.

- **Transference** – seeing your client as the same as a previous client, leading you to 'cut and paste' a previous package onto your new client. Everyone is different.

- **Projection** – throwing your fears, frustrations and preferences onto them. This, for example, could be a bias against them investing in property because this worked out badly for you recently.

- **Stereotyping** – making a judgement about another person based on such things as age, weight, occupation, skin colour, gender, etc.

There are many more biases that could affect the work of a financial adviser – you can check out a

comprehensive list of biases here: https://corporatefi-
nanceinstitute.com/resources/career-map/sell-side/
capital-markets/list-top-10-types-cognitive-bias.

Achieving this neutrality and focus isn't easy, but
a concept used in psychology is 'holding space'.
According to *Psychology Today,* this is the 'practice of
making space for somebody else's experience and cen-
tering [on] them.[15] To hold space, you must be fully
present and create a safe environment. Once the circumstances are created, holding space fosters listening
and empathizing.'

Mindfulness and meditative practices can help. The
authors of this book use a metaphor they call 'Settling
the Sand', and here's an image of the actual container
Cliff uses to demonstrate it.

© Emotional Intelligence Academy Ltd (2024)

The container on the right is filled with sand and water. When this is shaken and the sand mixes with the water, it resembles the image on the left. This represents what we are like when thoughts control us. We become so clogged up with thoughts that we can't see what we need to focus on. When you leave the container for two minutes, the sand settles, and it looks like the image on the right again, so that you can see clearly through the water in the top half of the glass.

When you are stressed or overthinking something, you can just give this container a shake, put it on the table and watch the sand settle. This will help you to settle the wandering thoughts going on in your mind, which are contaminating the process ahead. This is similar to a two-minute meditation practice which, as we are busy people, is probably all we can afford during our day, but it is an exercise that you will find helpful.

After a few months of using it, you won't need the prop any more, because you will visualise this automatically. Arrive at your meetings ahead of schedule, sit in the car and visualise the sand settling in the container to settle your mind. A 'calm mind' can help with what we call single-minded attention. By this we mean that you are not focusing on nothing; you are focusing on your clients, or on the project at hand. Mindfulness is simply single-minded attention.

Communication styles

The Emotional Intelligence Academy has developed a tool to help individuals identify their preferred communication styles.[16] This can be useful in helping us to connect with others by tuning into the others' style and using it rather than our own. In interactions with others, many of us have a bias towards one or more of the four styles, which are *empathic*, *critical*, *searching* and *advising*. Although the online assessment tool is useful, it is fairly easy to work out the preferred styles of others and, even more so, to work out our own from these general descriptors:

The empathic response

The empathic response is a nonjudgemental reply that captures the essential theme and/or feeling expressed. This communication response reflects a positive attitude and goes a long way in making communication a two-way exchange. It includes statements that reflect what the other is saying, thinking or feeling, such as:

- 'I can tell you are really pleased with your business success.'

- 'I can see that losing your partner is devastating for you.'

- 'You seem to be very comfortable with the balance of risk and security you have with this portfolio.'

You have to make sure your intention is to demonstrate that you understand what is going on for your client. If you get this wrong, it can backfire as it can show that you aren't listening or understanding their position. If you practise and master this style as your first response when others are sharing personal or emotional information, it can accelerate your rapport and trust-building efforts. We will come back to the value of empathic responses as we go through the client journey in this book.

The critical response

The critical response expresses judgement or evaluation that the other person can often perceive as a put-down. Such responses often result from a natural tendency to judge others, usually in a disapproving way. Examples might be:

- 'If you don't take risks and speculate, you will fail.'

- 'You don't understand finance, which is why I am here.'

- 'You would be a fool to go into property.'

Because a critical response is often perceived by the other person as a threat, it increases their emotional level and they may feel turned off, labelled and categorised. There are three unfortunate outcomes of the critical response: the other person (1) may feel rejected or put down, (2) they may not have a chance to release the feelings and emotions that may be begging for expression, and (3) they will often retreat or 'clam up'.

Many factors can lead us to make critical responses. One is the pressure of time and conflicting priorities (ie we have other things to do than listen to another person's problems). Another is that the other person's values and ideas may differ from our own, thus biasing us against them. Yet another is that we have our own experiences and needs, and in our desire to share these with others, we inadvertently adopt ways that are easily construed as being critical or judgemental. Being critical is often harmful and should be avoided at all costs unless you really know the person and the situation well and feel it will be valued by your client.

The searching response

The searching response asks for additional information. Sometimes we need more facts and figures if we are to understand the other person and their situation when we get into the data-gathering phase of the process. Having all the information will help us get to the best solution for the client. These are all good reasons for using a searching response, but there are times when a searching response, as an initial response, is inappropriate. Too many questions may signal that we weren't listening to the other person when they first explained their situation. It can also feel like an interrogation, giving clients a feeling that they are being 'grilled', or 'being given the third degree'. Sometimes, we want to help a client to 'ventilate' and thereby express their emotions and relevant factors that impact their wealth management. An empathic prompt is best, but a question designed to help the client share their information and feelings early in the relationship can be the next best thing in developing openness and flow.

Examples might include:

- Open questions using 'TED' (Tell me/Explain/ Describe) questions: 'Please tell me what is important to you'; 'Please explain how you approach savings and investments up to now'; 'Can you describe the position you would like to be in ten years from now?'

- 'What worries you most about the things we have discussed?'

- 'What do I need to do for you to be delighted with our relationship?'

Be careful with 'why' questions as they can come across as judgemental, even critical.

You can always come back to specific data gathering once the foundations of trust are in place.

The advising response

The advising response is one that offers a recommendation, suggesting what the client should or should not do. After all, that's what they are paying us for... right?

Well, yes and no. When we give another person advice, we deprive them of the chance to process or talk through what they are thinking and feeling. This kind of communication mode tends to build *dependent* relationships and can be more about us building our own sense of self-worth or status. The best help we can give others is to enable them to work out their own solutions by providing options and highlighting the risks and benefits of each. People feel more self-confident and behave more maturely (and independently) when they can plan and organise their own solutions rather than have others tell them what to do.

Ok... ok... this may go against what many people, including your clients, believe is a financial adviser's job, but if you reflect on your practice, you will see your successes come from you presenting options and letting the client buy into and own the solutions you reach together. It is tempting to respond when the client says, 'What would *you* do?' But you are not your client... Like doctors who are asked similar questions, professional consultants and advisers should always present options aligned to the client, not themselves. There is a personal liability/risk issue here, too, because if you push *your* advice and it doesn't work... it's *your* fault. Also, when we are busy thinking of solutions while the other person is speaking and processing ideas, we cannot listen fully to what they are saying. So, try to keep the advice monster in its cage.

So, empathic responses trump advising, searching and critical responses every time, as a *first* reaction. Try it the next time someone (a client, partner, friend, neighbour or family member) shares something emotional or something that matters to them. You will be judged by them to be caring and emotionally intelligent. Don't overdo it though – it can be seen as a manipulative tactic, or a little 'woo-woo' if overused.

Emotions, triggers and purposes

In Chapter 1, we discussed the seven core emotions. These emotions are designed to aid us. Each has a universal trigger and a function that has helped us to survive as a species. They also have sensations that are unique to each emotion. These are outlined in the table below, developed by Dr Paul Ekman and the Emotional Intelligence Academy.

Triggers, functions and sensations

	Surprise	Fear	Sadness	Happiness	Disgust	Contempt	Anger
Universal Trigger	Sudden and unexpected	Threat of harm	Loss of valued person/object	Pleasure	Offensive	Immoral action	Interference with goals
Function	Focuses attention	Avoid or reduce harm	Call for help. Time to recoup	Social sign of friendliness, discourage others' actions	Get away from trigger, block off nose or mouth	Assert own superiority	Stop interference, eliminate threat to goal
Sensation	Attentive	Cold, constricted, holding breath	Sore throat, aching/watery eyes	Warmth in whole body	Revulsion in mouth or throat	Feels superior (maybe happiness, disgust or anger)	Heat in upper body/face, pressure cooker, muscle tension

You can find out more about these emotions in Dr Paul Ekman's classic book *Emotions Revealed*.[17]

As an example, let's look at fear. The universal trigger for fear is the threat of harm to you or someone you care about. The function of that fear is to avoid or reduce that harm. The sensations that we will feel are cold, constricted and holding our breath.

There may be innate universal triggers for each emotion, but the cause of each emotion is unique to every individual. For example, the mention of the stock market to one client might trigger fear due to a negative experience they have had, whereas another client might feel pleasure or excitement as they are a risk-taker and enjoy the uncertainty the stock market offers.

Triggers can be learned from emotional and traumatic experiences which normally stay with us for life and can sometimes become phobias. The neuroscientist Joe LeDoux describes this as using a fish trap or a lobster pot, because once a trigger is learned it is very difficult to remove, often needing therapeutic support to enable us to deal with it in a more balanced way.[18] Therefore, if you see fear on your client's face, it's always wise to avoid jumping to conclusions about what is triggering that emotion for them. Remember, emotions can be triggered by your client's memories, certain words or thoughts. It may have nothing to do with what you are saying at the time.

Be conscious of the environment, too, because the time and place of your meetings could also affect your client.

While many triggers are unique, then, it's worth noting that there are some that universally evolved. Let's stay with fear for a moment. A large object moving towards you when you are driving may not be the same as a huge sabre-toothed tiger running towards our primate ancestors, but the fear is often the same. It causes our heart rate to rise. It charges our major organs like our lungs and our hearts to prepare us to escape the threat. The blood moves away from our skin surface to prevent blood loss in case we are injured, and our eyes widen to take in as much information as we can.

We will cover these emotional signals throughout the book, including the universal facial expressions that can flash across your client's (and your own) face even when we don't want to show each other our emotions.

How emotions affect decisions

When making decisions, consciously or otherwise, we might often predict how we may feel in the future and make our choices based on the avoidance of regret.[19] This is not to say we need to keep emotions out of decision making, it means that we need to understand how emotions can affect or bias our client's decision making during the investment savings decision-making process.

Predictions your client makes will be influenced by their thinking and their emotional state. When we're in a happy state or a positive frame of mind, we might more readily plan for the future and focus on the benefits of a given course of action. However, when we are anxious or in a pessimistic or negative frame of mind, we are more likely to focus on the present and the risks involved in any decision. These present-future time dimensions and risk-benefits analyses are core to financial decision making.

The emotionally intelligent financial adviser can read and influence the emotional state of the client to help them make the decisions needed to achieve their goals. You may, for example, want to suggest a break or to reschedule discussions that are crucial for the client to ensure the outcomes aren't contaminated by inappropriate emotions or mindsets that they are currently experiencing.

It is also worth noting that when our physical, cognitive and emotional resources are depleted, we are more likely to let our emotions drive our choices rather than use logic and reasoning. Figure 2.3 illustrates the competing demands for our resources.

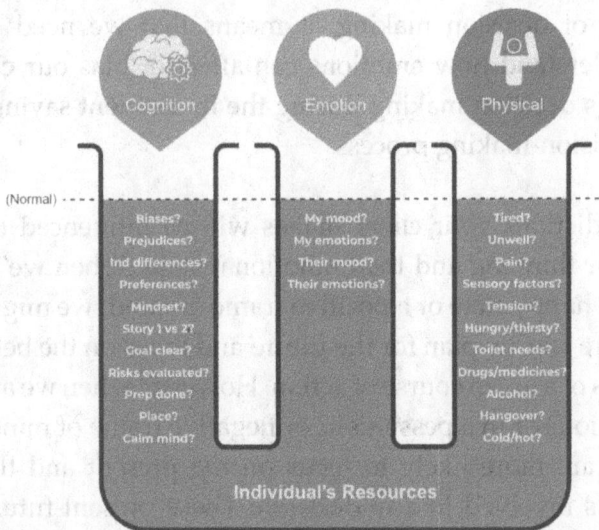

Cognition	Emotion	Physical
Biases?	My mood?	Tired?
Prejudices?	My emotions?	Unwell?
Ind differences?	Their mood?	Pain?
Preferences?	Their emotions?	Sensory factors?
Mindset?		Tension?
Story 1 vs 2?		Hungry/thirsty?
Goal clear?		Toilet needs?
Risks evaluated?		Drugs/medicines?
Prep done?		Alcohol?
Place?		Hangover?
Calm mind?		Cold/hot?

Individual's Resources

© Emotional Intelligence Academy Ltd (2024)

Here, the individual's resources are represented in each test tube by the liquid. We have limited resources, and we get daily draws on these depending on what is going on around us. The three tubes deal with:

- **Cognition** – our thoughts. Consider your client's mindset, biases and prejudices, for example. Are the time and the place distractions competing for their thinking resources? The concept of 'Story 1 or 2', developed by the Emotional Intelligence Academy, is a reminder that our initial interpretation (the 'Story 1' (bad story) we are telling ourselves about the client) may be mistaken – there may be a 'Story 2' (good) reason behind their behaviour, and this reframing can help us to stay curious, rather than judgemental. Have they got a calm mind? Have you got a calm mind? Remember, this is about checking your thoughts too.

- **Emotions** – our feelings. According to the neuroscientist John LeDoux, in his book *The Emotional Brain*, we react emotionally around four times quicker than we respond cognitively. Emotions will therefore trump thinking every time.[20] They just involve the emotional brain and decisions are triggered without thought. They are unbidden. They happen to us, and if they aren't constructive and we are not able to interrupt them, think things through and come up with a rational, sensible solution, then often our decisions could be faulty.

- **Physical** – what is happening to us physically. Is your client tired, hungry, unwell? If they have such physical demands, then they are more likely to make a decision based primarily on this state and the associated mood and emotions they are feeling. This can lead to poor decisions.

Take care though. As skilled, curious observers of our client's behaviour, we may not know immediately what they are thinking, but we can hypothesise whether they are experiencing any strong emotions, and ask questions to determine the degree to which those emotions are influencing their decisions.

Research examples

In 2011, a study of 1,112 judicial rulings from eight judges showed how depleted resources may affect decision making.[21] The majority of the decisions in the study were requests for parole being heard in the court. What was interesting was that the time a decision was made affected the outcome. Each day, the judges had two breaks for food, which segmented the day into three distinct sessions. The researchers found that favourable decisions dropped gradually from around 65% at the beginning of the session to nearly zero towards the end. After the break, the favourable decisions returned to an average of 65%. So, what was happening?

It's difficult to say specifically, but we can hypothesise that hunger, toilet needs or fatigue may have influenced the judges' decisions. The researchers themselves stated that they did not measure the judges' moods or mental resources, but they agreed that it was likely that the judges were susceptible to psycho-physiological biases.

Thinking about the test-tube model in Figure 2.3, when our physical or emotional needs demand our attention, that leaves fewer resources available for cognition. Which, in the case of the judges, may have resulted in a bias in their decision making.

Rapport and trust

The aim of rapport building is to create trust, and you need to think about this in advance of your first meeting with a new client. When we are careful with, and pay attention to, a response and the emotional needs of others, trust grows. When we don't, it can damage trust. Trust can be defined as, 'a psychological state comprising the intention to accept vulnerability based upon positive expectations of the intentions or behaviour of another.'[22]

Everything a financial adviser does for their clients is based on trust being firmly established. They are often relying on you to help them achieve their life goals, their dreams, their needs and wants – they are entrusting everything they have to the investment solutions you are presenting to them.

So, rapport is important. It is useful to remember that we like people who are like us, so it's always good to find a common interest. If you meet someone you have something in common with, you can leverage this to build a connection with them. It is important to pick up on this common ground early in your interaction with a client. This will help you build rapport. This common ground could be liking the same sports team, for example, so that you can talk about the game played at the weekend. Maybe you notice photographs, images and trophies as you walk into their office or home that you can comment on. Maybe you both played hockey as teenagers, or you like pets, sailing or motorcycles. Once you find something you are both interested in, you become part of the same tribe. This is very powerful. The minute you have some common ground, it massively puts free credits into the trust account and, if you can do that early in the interaction, it sets you up for success.

We've all had that experience where you meet someone for the first time and, just in casual conversation, you realise you have lots in common and suddenly you feel like you are friends. It happens unconsciously. Identifying similar preferences, interests or values is powerful for relationship building.

It is a way of introducing small talk, and finding common interests can be a lubricant for social communication and is a good method of building rapport. We will go into this in more detail in the next chapter which deals with how best to use casual conversations and prompts to help you build rapport and trust with your client.

A climate for information gathering

When we have rapport and trust with someone, we feel comfortable sharing. Financial advisers require information to do their job effectively. The client needs to be comfortable sharing personal financial details, goals and aspirations. If you don't feel the client is disclosing, ask yourself, 'Have I built rapport and have I earned their trust?' If not, you have some work to do.

But it is important to remember that if you push too hard you may damage the relationship. Don't become an interrogator. The client may not be ready and it is probably a sign that they don't trust you yet, so you will have to work harder.

We will provide you with elicitation models, tactics and tips in the next chapters to help you build rapport and trust quickly and effectively. This will then lay the foundation for the initial meeting, the planning meeting, the implementation stage, and your ongoing service work with your clients.

CASE STUDY: Like old friends

When James was training to be an adviser, he was on an academy programme. Part of that involved observing client meetings. At one such meeting with a very experienced adviser in a bank, James sat in the corner taking notes and watching what happened as the meeting unfolded. The client wanted to discuss what to do with their savings and was meeting the adviser for the first time. The meeting lasted about an hour.

What struck James was that the adviser and the client were like two old friends. They took an interest in each other. They discussed interests, hobbies, preferences and things that they'd been up to in life. The adviser leaned in at the right times and showed that she was listening, nodding at the right times, sighing at the right times, laughing at the right times, and showing sympathy and empathy at the right times. At the end of the meeting, the client sat back and said, 'Look, just let me know what you think I should do with this. I trust your advice.'

The success of the meeting was due to the interest the adviser took in the client building trust through sharing stories and finding connections.

But what was even more important was what the adviser didn't do.

She didn't spend the time talking about investments and the different options that are available to the client, or the features and advantages of each of those options, and she didn't spend most of the time talking about herself. What James observed was a financial adviser skilled in holding space, leaning in appropriately, and getting curious about the other person in a natural way, which resulted in a trusting relationship.

Skill builder

The aim of this 'skill builder' is to think about how emotions and their learned triggers affect the decisions that we and our clients make around money.

1. Think of a time when you felt a particular emotion when dealing with a client. What emotion was that?

2. Consider the universal theme (or trigger) for that emotion.

3. Ask yourself the following questions:

- Where does this emotion come from?

- What prior experience or learning is behind this thinking?

- Did you learn this from how your parents behaved around money?

- Was that the trigger?

- What was their behaviour around money?

- Were they wasteful or cautious?

- How did the session(s) work out?

- How can you manage this in the future?

- How can you interrupt the trigger?

- Knowing what you know now, what could you have done better in your interaction with that client?

Summary

Understanding and managing emotional triggers is crucial for financial advisers. These triggers, often rooted in past experiences, can impact your success if not addressed. This chapter has explored how emotional triggers affect decision making, emphasising that your attitude, feelings and thoughts towards clients are communicated through subtle signals in your face, body and voice. Clients pick up on these subconscious cues, making it difficult to hide your true feelings, which can inadvertently reveal judgements or strong emotions you are harbouring about your client.

This chapter has also delved into mindsets and biases, highlighting the key biases of Me-Theory, Transference, Projection and Stereotyping. Recognising these biases will help you adopt a more effective approach: cultivating a curious mindset to better understand your clients' behaviour. We identified four key communication styles – empathic, critical, searching and advising – that can enhance interactions with clients.

Building rapport and trust is fundamental; paying close attention to a client's emotional needs fosters trust, while neglecting them can damage it. Trust is the foundation of a financial adviser's relationship with their clients.

Ultimately, rapport is crucial. By addressing and managing emotional triggers, adopting a curious mindset, and focusing on building trust through attentive and empathetic communication, you can significantly enhance your client relationships and boost your overall success.

THREE
Preparing For Action

O nce you have a prospect lined up, your first instinct may be to find out what you can about them and arrange an initial meeting to take stock of their situation – their assets, income, dreams and wants. Before you do that, however, it's worth pausing for a moment and checking out where you are.

As a professional, you'll be up to date with the financial products and services that you offer, and you'll be aware of legislation or government policy changes. Your client will expect that. It's also best to check the press and internet for any crises or economic-related announcements on the morning of your meeting.

We also advise that you don't check your emails before a meeting, because there may be something there that will put you in the wrong mindset. It could be a complaint from a client, for example, which could steal your focus during the meeting rather than attending to the client in front of you.

In advance of this first meeting, you would also be wise to reflect on the mindset and biases section in the previous chapter. If you are aware of any of these that push you towards or away from certain products, people or situations, then half the battle is recognising those biases and preferences. You then need to work hard to suspend your own preferences and biases as they may conflict with the goals, preferences, wants and needs of your client.

This can be challenging, especially if you have a major problem with a recent client or product, or had a huge success with a certain product in another similar situation. Such outcomes can increase or decrease our confidence in a certain area and lead to bias, keeping us within a certain comfort zone.

It can help you to make a note at this point of these biases. Take a moment to ask yourself the following questions:

- What recent situations/clients have been really successful/challenging?

- How could these affect my confidence/ preferences?

- What do I need to think about if I face similar contexts in the future?

Check your tubes

It's well worth reflecting on the triple test-tube metaphor we used in the last chapter. Consider the factors on each of the three test tubes and note the questions below to identify if you have any cognitive, emotional and/or physical demands on your personal resources that you need to deal with before you meet your client. Take a moment before the initial meeting to ask yourself the following questions:

- What cognitive/emotional/physical elements are not optimal for me to engage with the client? Eg are you tired? Do you need to use the bathroom? Have you prepared enough?

- How might these affect your performance/ advice?

- What do I need to do to address these elements before I meet my client?

Take whatever action you need to ensure that you are in the best mindset and state possible before you sit down at the table with your client.

It's not all about me?

You are the financial expert, and your client has come to you because you have been recommended to them or you have caught their attention through your promotional activity. However, you need to be careful that you don't approach your initial client meeting with a mindset that 'you know best'. If you are an angler with a liking for vanilla-filled doughnuts, you don't bait your hook with them because you think the fish should prefer them over worms. You may have to suspend your likes and preferences and bait the hook with a worm to suit the fish. By doing this, you demonstrate that you considered what the client may want and need.

This means adopting an open and curious mindset with an initial goal of fully understanding your client's situation, their likes, fears, goals and dreams. Therefore, how, when and where you meet should be geared to your client's preferences.

We like meeting clients in our offices. It's convenient. It shows off our certificates. The coffee's great and we have access to all our documentation. Some people are, however, like Cliff's mother. Soon after Cliff lost his father, his mother needed help getting their business and affairs in order. Zoom was out of the question. She hates technology and it would signal, Cliff thought, that he didn't have enough time to visit her. He didn't even contemplate it. If he wanted to have serious discussions with his mother, then, for it to be successful, she had to be comfortable. That meant that the best time of day was mid-afternoon so he could sample her latest baking achievement and share a pot of tea with her while sitting around her kitchen table. He could have tried meeting her at his office, at his home, in the coffee shop, or at the local garden centre that she loved, but she wouldn't be at ease with having important discussions in those environments. His mother's kitchen it was then.

Post-COVID, it can be so easy to avoid the traffic and the train delays by simply coercing the client to use email or meet via Zoom or Teams. Plus, it means we can get two or three clients covered in a day rather than one. Some clients may prefer a remote meeting for their own convenience or circumstances, though we see too many service providers forcing this option onto clients. In many cases, it's selfish. Instead, ask your client where they want to meet. They may say they want to meet in person. Remember, it's not all about us.

You never get a second chance to make a first impression

Whether your initial contact is by email, phone, live chat, letter, Zoom or face-to-face, take a moment to check the test tubes that we explored earlier and make sure you are in the right cognitive, emotional and physical state to handle these first contacts successfully.

If you focus 100% on a client and seek to understand them, you simply need to listen, stay curious and be empathic. This can begin before your first interaction by researching what you can about them. Check Facebook, LinkedIn and the wider internet to see if you can discover a little about their life, business, relationships and hobbies.

You need to be careful not to let this bias your contact with any prejudgements, but it can give you some ideas that will help you connect and build rapport with your client. You may notice, for example, that they have a pet, a hobby or a connection that you share. Common ground is great for helping the flow of your early conversations. Take care when you are actually in the meeting, to let them lead if it appears that they have a clear agenda. Otherwise, this demonstration of your extensive research may make you appear to be a little desperate.

When developing your brand and image, you may have to suspend your love of denims and AC/DC t-shirts and think about what clients may expect from a professional financial adviser. Times are changing from the days when most business professionals wore a formal suit. Nowadays, there is a risk of overdressing and making the client feel uncomfortable. Our rule of thumb is to make sure we are dressed one level up on the client – if they wear suits and no scarf/cravat/ tie, we may add the formal accessory – if they wear 'smart casual', we may go with a suit without any formal neckwear – if they turn up in denims and a t-shirt, you might dress down a little to smart/casual if your formality is creating a barrier.

Obviously, you will have to guess the likely clothing choices of the client for the first meeting until you gauge whether you can dress down a little for the next meeting. But some clients will judge you by your clothes. Cliff deals with many military and law enforcement professionals and, therefore, for those meetings, he always makes sure his clothing is formal and well-pressed and his (black) shoes are pristine and highly polished. That's because many folks from the Services will judge a person on their attire and shoes. The same goes for your email, documents, website and social media. Financial clients will need to see stability and professionalism in all that you present to them if they are to trust you with their assets and future plans.

James deals with many clients who are lawyers, so he wears a three-piece suit and tie. But if he is going to go to see an elderly client at their home, such formality can be intimidating.

Your brand isn't all about what you wear, either. Take, for example, a financial adviser who might hire a driver when he visits a hedge-fund manager who probably has millions to invest so as to influence the way in which he is seen by the client when he arrives. If that same adviser arrives at old Mrs Meakin's house down the road to talk about her pension pot, she will immediately be put off by the sight of a financial adviser arriving at her house in a chauffeur-driven car – clearly making too much profit!

Reliability is key too. Never, ever, ever be late for a client meeting. There are no reasons for being late unless there's been a major accident or death in the family. Lateness essentially means, 'I chose to prioritise something else over you, my client.' This sounds tough, but professionals will build contingencies for almost all eventualities. Traffic, accidents, weather, train strikes, broken alarm clocks and getting lost.

The live data available to us these days can help us to decide whether we should aim to get there an hour early and have a coffee at the client's end of the journey rather than before we leave home. You might even consider leaving home the evening before and staying overnight. Many of us have families, pets and other responsibilities and this is not always easy, though you'll be emotionally intelligent and successful enough to have a good circle of friends and support to help you in times of need.

Being on time means arriving at the client's location at least fifteen minutes before the appointment time, so make sure you use a bathroom, check your clothing, turn off your phone and notifications, collect your thoughts, do a quick test-tube scan and give yourself two minutes to settle the sand before you meet your clients. Treat each meeting as if your life depends on it as, for some of your clients, it does for them.

On the steps – mindset and focus

Now that you have arrived at the venue to meet the client or are about to click the Zoom/Teams link for your virtual meeting, it is time to remind yourself of the mindset and focus that will help you and your clients succeed. Take the following steps:

1. Do a test-tube scan and fix what you can.

2. Be ready to allow the client to speak for 80% of the time.

3. Be curious and avoid judgement.

4. Make your initial responses during your meeting empathic. Do not advise, criticise or avoid questions.

5. Be ready to look and listen for clues as to what's going on beneath the surface of their words.

The iceberg model below shows that you are not just listening to the words the client uses. Explore and listen for the meaning, their thinking and the feeling behind the words and get tuned into any deeper principles emerging to do with the client's values and beliefs that you need to pay attention to. Only then can you truly empathise with your client.

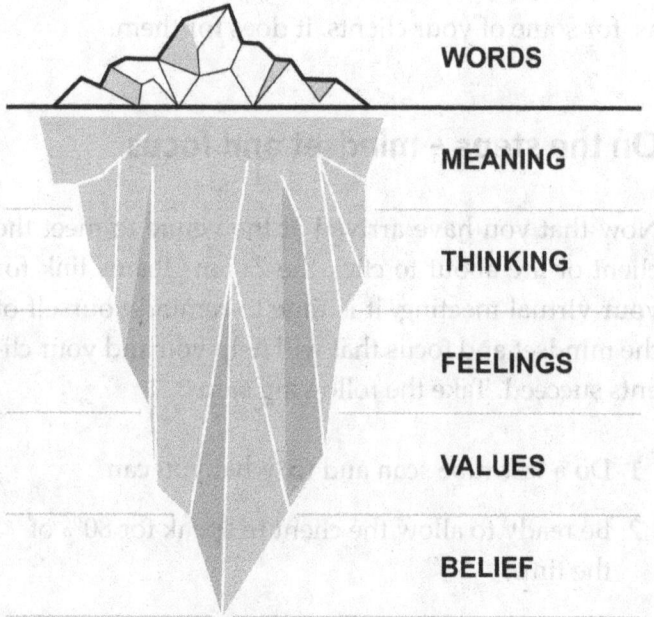

WORDS

MEANING

THINKING

FEELINGS

VALUES

BELIEF

© *Emotional Intelligence Academy Ltd (2024)*

CASE STUDY: Meeting roadblocks

James should have listened to his client when she said she would come to meet him at his office for their initial meeting. It would have taken her twenty minutes by train. Instead, thinking it would make a good impression on her, he set off driving the ten miles across London to her home. Inevitably, he hit delay after delay and ended up being an hour late for their meeting. By the time he got there, his client was leaving for work. It wasn't as though he hadn't checked how long it was going to take, it was just the traffic. The client was not happy. She did, however, agree to reschedule the meeting. Again, she said she would come to his office, but James refused to hear any of it. On the day of the rescheduled meeting, he left even earlier, but within a few minutes, he was stuck in a queue of traffic and late again!

This time it broke the relationship. James had to pass the client to another financial adviser in the business as she refused to deal with him any longer.

While giving a good impression was the aim here, by not listening to the client and failing to allow for the travel difficulties, the opposite was achieved. It can be important to suspend our own ideas and beliefs and listen to our clients.

Skill builder

In this exercise, we want to build your resilience as a financial adviser. Going back to the test-tube diagram above, ask yourself the following questions:

- What cognitive and physical elements, such as tiredness, hunger or pain, tend to affect you more than the others?

- How has this affected you and your clients in the past?

Note down an action plan that will help you to build resilience and habits that will help manage this.

Summary

In this chapter, we have helped you prepare for your first interaction with your client. We have considered:

- Exploring and handling your own biases and preferences

- Carrying out a test-tube scan to see how your cognitive, emotional and physical state may help or hinder your work

- Focusing on your client's needs, wants, preferences and goals, and making a good first impression

- Getting yourself into the right mindset for your first client meeting

Now that you have fully prepared for your initial meeting, the next chapter will look at what you need to do to ensure that meeting is effective and successful for you and your client.

FOUR

Initial Meeting

I n 1997, Arthur Aron and colleagues conducted a series of experiments designed to investigate closeness between individuals.[23] The experiment involved pairs of participants asking each other a series of thirty-six questions. These questions started at a surface level, like the *FORCED* 'small talk' model we will discuss later in this chapter, and then proceeded to deeper, personal questions, and finally to emotional questions. The participants were encouraged to mutually share if appropriate.

The results of the study showed that these types of questions created a sense of trust and intimacy within a short amount of time. Being vulnerable in the presence of another creates a sense of trust, which builds strong foundations for a relationship. Importantly, the findings of the study have been replicated, indicating that they may be reliable. In one interesting replication, participants had a discussion with an AI using the thirty-six questions and showed that the same closeness and trust could be formed with a nonhuman participant.[24] The finding that closeness can be created between a human and an AI shows the power of asking the right questions.

In this chapter, we will look at client interactions starting with the initial meeting. As we previously mentioned, you will have your own way of structuring these meetings, so our aim is not to teach you new ways, but to show you a framework we use to demonstrate where EI skills and abilities can be applied to improve success with your clients. We suggest that you take the learning in this chapter and apply it to your own ways of working, in your own business or the company that you work for.

The aim of the initial meeting is to find out, based on what the client tells you, whether you can help them achieve their financial goals. Likewise, your potential client needs to know whether you are the right fit for them, and if you are not then we advise that you recommend where they can go to have their needs better met. The initial meeting is therefore only an exercise in exploring whether you are going to work together.

Some clients may not have worked with an adviser before and may be nervous due to the unfamiliar situation they find themselves in. Others may have preconceptions due to their previous experience with advisers. Consequently, it is important to be aware of these signals and be ready to reassure the client, or to be assertive if they are trying to direct the meeting early on.

Best practice is to agree on the purpose of the meeting early with the client – namely, that it is to see if you want to work together, and if so, what the next steps will be. This takes the pressure off nervous clients who may think they must make decisions about where to invest money on that particular day.

This sets the agenda and helps you retain focus, as some clients may want to wrestle that from you because they have their own agenda and want to direct the meeting from the beginning. It's a balance between the client feeling in control and you using your experience to keep the process safe, efficient and productive for your client.

The initial meeting works best using a consultative selling approach where the adviser allows the client to do most of the talking, and questions are used to help the client share their goals, hopes and fears, and to keep the conversation flowing.

Then, once you have gathered enough information about the client and their wants and needs, you can finish the meeting by summarising their position and linking your service proposition to their aims and objectives and explaining how your service is going to fit their needs. However, as we've said before, if your service is not right, be prepared to point them elsewhere where they can get help.

Engaging the client

When we engage with people, information is exchanged through words and behaviour across six communication channels. This is drawn from the 'SCANS' system and is summarised here:[25]

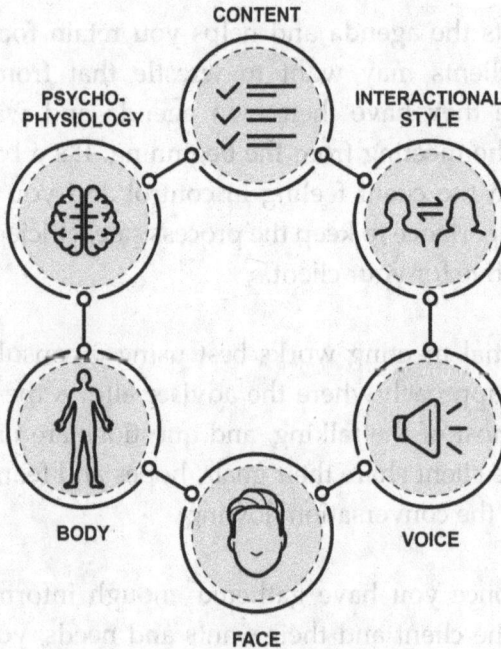

CONTENT

PSYCHO-PHYSIOLOGY

INTERACTIONAL STYLE

BODY

VOICE

FACE

© Emotional Intelligence Academy Ltd (2024)

- **Face:** We use our face to communicate many things, including how we are feeling. Each emotion introduced in Chapter 1 has a universal facial expression. These can be very quick and subtle, which we call micro-expressions.

- **Body:** We use gestures to communicate, and our posture or body position can also convey information.

- **Psychophysiology:** Emotions affect our physiology. For example, heart rate increases or breathing rate changes. Although subtle, you may be able to pick up on these.

- **Content:** What our clients are saying. Our word choices can give clues that we are experiencing strong emotion.

- **Voice:** The pitch, tone, speed and volume of speech.

- **Interactional style:** How we interact, the flow of the conversation, and how pauses, or fillers, like umm, erm, are used in conversation.

When you meet a client, it is useful to pay attention to all these channels. It can be a little challenging to be aware of all six channels at once, though once you have picked up the key cues we will cover in this book, you will be surprised at how often you notice signals that tell you what a person is feeling and thinking.

You might miss a change in the tone or volume of the client's voice in the early days because you are concentrating on what is happening with their facial expressions. However, in time you will be able to read, understand and influence others skilfully using such signals. In the short term, you may find it helpful to record the conversations (with proper permissions/use), so that you can review and pick out these details later. Whether you meet the client face-to-face or virtually, it's worth asking the client's permission to record the meeting. If they agree, you can then do this either by using a voice recorder if you are face-to-face, or using the record functions within virtual meetings such as Zoom or Teams. Following the meeting, you might then use technology and AI to transcribe and summarise meetings – even develop actions for you. As your back-office support team won't be at the meeting (if you have such a team), they will applaud you for recording the meeting because this makes handovers to other colleagues far easier.

Rapport building

We began discussing rapport in Chapter 2, and now, in this chapter, we will build on that. Rapport refers to a positive state in relationships where both parties communicate well and respect and understand each other. Building rapport is the first step to establishing trust with your prospective client. Therefore, adequate time needs to be allocated in every meeting for rapport building because when rapport is in place, conversations flow easily. Financial advisors' and financial planners' roles are based on being a trusted adviser in the client's lives. The quicker you can establish that trust, the easier your job will be. Rapport building is best done at the beginning of the meeting. Some might call it small talk but, while that is a fair description, don't downplay its value.

It is important to be aware that there are cultural differences when it comes to rapport. Getting down to business too quickly can be frowned upon in some cultures, such as in Japan or many Middle Eastern countries. On the other hand, a quicker approach is often valued in Scandinavia or Germany. These are only broad generalisations – everyone is different – and you need to read the client and the situation, and judge whether they welcome your small talk or not and move on when you need to.

It is also vital to remember the six channels of communication to help build rapport. Listen and watch carefully for the volume of their voice, the rate of their speech, the gestures they use, how they use language and how they interact with you. For example, if someone regularly uses your name, that might be their style. If you then match that style using their name more often in conversation, this will promote better rapport between you. This is sometimes referred to as 'mirroring'.

If you are meeting your client face-to-face at your office, for example, then rapport building starts in the lobby when you meet the client, and as you walk with them to the meeting room. These small conversations that take place before and after meetings are very important for forming trust and relationship building.

Here are some simple ways to begin building rapport with your client:

- Use their name.
- Shake their hand.
- Find common ground.
- Use context references – eg 'The weather has changed for the better today.'
- Offer some information about yourself to get information back.

FORCED model for rapport

To some, rapport building comes naturally. They are good at making small talk and building rapport is not something that they need to give too much thought to. If that's not you, though, and you feel that you need some help structuring your initial conversations with prospective clients, the FORCED model for rapport building will help.

FORCED was designed for use by undercover air marshals to help them engage people of interest to decide whether they are a security threat – the results are impressive.[26] FORCED is built around the following topics:

- Family/friends
- Occupation
- Recreation
- Current events
- Education/skills
- Dreams/plans

You can use statements, prompts and questions (such as how, what, when, where, who, tell me, explain, describe) to explore these topics with your client so that you can start building rapport before you move on to business matters. It's wise to avoid 'why' questions, as they can sometimes come across as judgemental.

Here are some examples:

- **Family:** Is that your family in the photo?
- **Occupation:** What do you do for work? Oh, you're a landscaper. Tell me a bit more about that.

- **Current events:** What do you think about what's going on in politics right now?

- **Recreation:** What do you do on the weekends when you're not working?

Testing rapport

How do you know when rapport has been established? Some markers for rapport were mentioned in the case study in Chapter 2 about the bank's financial adviser and their client – laughing together, empathy, listening, mutual interest and attention to each other, and the easy flow of conversation. If you notice these markers in your initial meeting with your client, then it's likely that you are 'in rapport'.

Also, consider the level of disclosure. When we are in rapport, we feel safe disclosing information, even to someone that we have just met. But if your prospective client is not disclosing, take a step back to less personal ground. Move away from personal questions as you may be going too deep too quickly. Keep the conversation light.

You may be familiar with the concept of *matching* and *mirroring* which will also help you test if you are in rapport with your client. When people are in rapport, they tend to match and mirror each other's pace and tone of voice, body language, postures and gestures. As a test, you could change your posture, for example, leaning back in your chair, and if your prospective client mirrors you with their body language, then this is a marker of successful rapport as it indicates that your client feels comfortable in your presence and with the conversation. If you are having a video meeting, you might move closer to your camera if your client is close to their camera. However, be aware of the risks here because if the client realises you are copying their body language, this may damage the interaction as they will think you are mimicking them and you will lose their trust.

You can also consider the speed of a client's speech. They may be fast talkers or talk more slowly due to regional sociolect/variances. If you can get closer to the pace of their speech it will be a subtle way to build rapport.

Deeper conversations – The Trusted Adviser Method™

The closeness experiment introduced at the beginning of this chapter demonstrated that the right question, asked at the right time, is critical in building trust quickly in relationships. The Trusted Adviser Method (TA Method)™ builds on the FORCED model and applies the concept of asking successive questions of increasing depth, combined with appropriate mutual disclosure, in financial planning scenarios. The model is a guide to help you formulate and ask questions which invite your client to be more open. In doing so, you create an opportunity to connect deeply with your client, solidifying the relationship at an early stage. The questioning technique also has the capacity to elicit emotion in your client, so be careful, keep it safe for them, pay attention and be ready to respond. Recognising and responding to your client's emotions appropriately will demonstrate that you understand them.

The TA Method™ uses a framework of open questions combined with financial themes and words for eliciting fears, goals, satisfaction and preferences. You can construct your own questions, or if you go to Appendix 1, or follow the QR code below, you can access a set of fifty-four questions we have created for you.

How to construct questions using the model

Starting with an open question will give your client an opportunity to share information. Avoid asking questions where the answer is yes/no as the aim here is to get your client to think about their answer and provide you with detail.

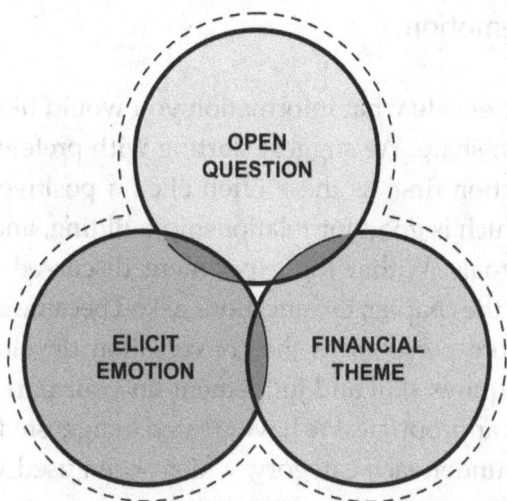

If you recall from the FORCED model, good questions start with what, where, when, who, how, tell, explain or describe.

Financial themes

Once you have settled on an opener, decide on a theme. We have created a range of themes here around financial planning, but you could create more if you feel there are any missing:

retirement, investing, family, home, education, tax planning, business (if an owner), work, career, lifestyle, spending, debt (including mortgage), friends, hobbies, health, fitness, spirituality, giving and charity.

Elicit emotion

Finally, decide what information you would like your client to share. We suggest starting with preferences/ satisfaction first, as these often elicit a positive emotion which is good for relationship building, and then fears/goals. Within the experiment discussed at the start of the chapter, the questions asked became deeper and more personal as the conversation developed.[27] This requires skill and judgement on your part about what is appropriate. We have created a suggested list of words under each category, which when used within a question are designed to elicit a response from the client, providing you with rich information about the client's goals, fears, preferences, likes and dislikes:

- **For exploring fears:** Concerned/worry/anxious/ risk/secure/safe

- **For understanding goals:** Aspire/dream/goal/ envision/hope/wish/plan/heading

- **For gauging satisfaction:** Satisfied/content/ happy/frustrated/disappointed/pleased

- **For discussing preferences:** Prefer/like/ comfortable/inclined/interested/value

Once judgement is made, it is appropriate to ask more personal questions. Increase the depth as the conversation develops but watch out for signs of discomfort in your client and pull back if appropriate. Here are some general tips:

- Start broad, then narrow to get to the specifics.

- Listen intently. Let the client talk without interruption. This will allow your client to think through their answers.

- Reassure the client that your conversations are confidential. This will help with disclosure.

- Use empathy in response to answers, especially in the early stages, acknowledging the emotions you observe if appropriate.

- Share your personal experiences too, if appropriate, but don't hijack the conversation with your own stories – it's not about you.

The TA Method™ has been designed to replicate the experience participants had in the Aron study.[28] By harnessing the power of openness, vulnerability and mutual sharing, the model is a potent tool to help you gain your prospective clients' trust quickly. The questions are designed to touch upon the universal triggers of emotions, which will give you an opportunity to notice and respond to the client's behaviour. Here are some example questions to demonstrate how to use the model.

1. How satisfied are you with your current retirement plan?

2. What concerns do you have about your retirement plans?

3. What aspirations do you have for your or your family's educational future?

You can see the questions require some creative work on your part, but if you would like a shortcut, check out the appendix for a list of questions we have created for you.

Using the questions in the model gives you an opportunity to pay attention to the emotion in your client's responses. Often, emotion comes with discussing personal events or our plans, and a common one is sadness, which we will look at now.

Sadness

When sadness is experienced, it looks something like this:

© Emotional Intelligence Academy Ltd (2024)

Trigger: Loss of something or someone of value.

Purpose: Sadness is a call for help or to be left alone. Not all people experiencing sadness want to be helped; they may be ashamed of showing weakness. You need to judge when to support someone and when to leave them alone.

Face: Inner brows up and lip corners down.

Other behaviours: Voice pitch and volume drop, voice can break, loss of muscle tone, relaxing of posture.

Care: Observing the signs of sadness won't tell you what the client is sad about. You need to work that out and decide how to respond. If you see subtle signs, the client may be masking the emotion, and they may think it's an invasion of their privacy if you make them aware of your knowledge of something they are trying to hide. Sadness can also turn into anger directed at the person or thing that has caused the loss.

Responses: Show empathy, give them space, be patient, offer support (if appropriate), consider matching their speech volume and pitch, acknowledge the emotion (if appropriate) and offer to defer the meeting if needed. Some think it is useful to 'cheer them up' or tell them a joke. This often fails. You might want to check out this clip from the animated film *Inside Out* for an example of 'sadness saving the day' – www. youtube.com / watch?v=QT6FdhKriB8.

Refractory period

This is a good time to discuss an aspect of emotion we haven't yet looked at. There is a period following an emotional experience where our thoughts are influenced by the emotion. This is called a *refractory period* during which we tend to only take in information which supports the emotion we have just experienced, and our thoughts can be coloured by this.

This becomes like an emotional confirmation bias, where information from our environment is filtered. In the case of sadness, for example, we can be biased towards that emotion and may view information we take in through a 'loss lens'. A refractory period can last far longer than the emotion, which is often brief, and can even re-trigger the emotion. You see this with sadness, where people are overwhelmed, compose themselves, and then a short time later experience the emotion again. Following an emotional episode, you or your client may not return to the baseline you or they were previously at. It's a little like a recovery period after an exerting exercise routine. Be aware of this, as it can contaminate your interactions.

If you notice that the client may be in a refractory period, it might be wise to change the subject for a while, take a break, or even offer to defer a meeting which involves making plans. You will show a deep level of understanding of your client and their needs by providing this space, so don't be afraid to do so.

Contracting

After you and your prospective client have built rapport, and you have elicited information about their hopes and fears, you should have enough information to determine whether you can help them.

Take some time towards the end of the meeting to demonstrate that you have been listening by summarising your understanding of their position and reassuring them that you can meet the wants and needs which came out of the elicitation stage. Alternatively, be prepared to say that you cannot meet their needs and refer them to someone who can.

Summarising the client's position in their own words is a great way of building trust. You have shown you have listened and, by replaying their own words back to them, you are also proving to them you understand their position.

Once you have gained agreement to work together, you can formalise the agreement by contracting and discussing fees. Fee negotiations happen at the end of the initial meeting when it is clear to both parties what the general scope of work may be.

They are a prime opportunity to look for emotional clues that can provide signals about the client's intention to proceed. Nods of agreement and displays of emotions such as happiness should give you clues that the client is willing, whereas other emotions (such as anger, fear, disgust and contempt – see later) may suggest you need to work harder to convince the client and demonstrate the value you will provide. If the fee proposal is sudden and unexpected, this may trigger a brief display of surprise. Let's have a look at this emotion next.

Surprise

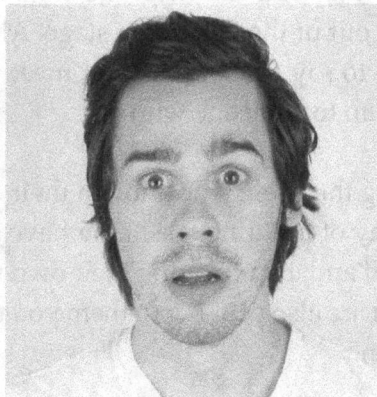

© Emotional Intelligence Academy Ltd (2024)

Trigger: Something sudden/unexpected.

Purpose: Helps us respond to unexpected events.

Face: Inner and outer brows lift, eyes wide, lips part/ jaw dropped. Genuine surprise only shows on the face for one or two seconds, as it usually morphs into another emotion like fear, happiness, anger, etc.

Other behaviours: Inhalations, slight pause, move away.

Care: Watch for surprise turning into another emotion. It is a transitory emotion, revealing a person is evaluating what is going on.

Responses: Hypothesise what the trigger may have been, acknowledge the surprise, clarify, give the client a moment to process the information, gauge their reaction, address any concerns, and provide reassurance.

Surprise in fee discussions

If you notice surprise when discussing your fees, it may mean the client wasn't expecting the cost – either because it's too high or too low. Here is a worked example of how to respond:

- Acknowledge/empathise – 'I see this fee might not be what you were expecting.'

- Clarify – 'Let me explain the costs a bit further.'

- Take a moment – 'Take your time, let me know any questions you have.'

- Respond – 'How do you feel now?'

- Concerns – 'What concerns do you have?

- Reassure – 'My priority is your financial well-being, and I'm committed to working with you to ensure my services are beneficial and affordable for you.'

The initial surprise can either be negative ('I wasn't expecting that much') or positive ('That's lower than I expected'). Your response will need to change depending on which it is.

CASE STUDY: Tears, tea and trust

Many years ago, James met with a new client who had recently lost his wife. The client was unsure what to do with the money he had inherited from an insurance policy and was seeking advice from the company James was working for.

In their first meeting, James reassured him that they would not be making any decisions that day and that they would take as much time as they needed to explore options and leave decisions for another day.

Several times in the meeting the client broke down crying. James offered support, which was mainly in the form of tea and periods of silence to allow the client time for reflection. James avoided interrupting or talking just for the sake of it as he didn't feel he could add any words that would resolve the emotion. Because of the sensitive way James dealt with the client, their two-hour meeting was the start of an eleven-year professional relationship, no doubt due to the trust established in this first meeting by responding to the emotions of the client in an appropriate way.

Skill builder

The exercise for this chapter is to use the TA Method conversation model on a friend or colleague.

Practise creating and using questions and gain feedback from your chosen participant on how they found the exercise.

Remember, start with surface-level questions, and deepen as you progress.

Summary

In this chapter, we have learned how to:

- Build rapport early in the meeting to establish a connection

- Listen actively to understand the client's concerns, needs and goals

- Deepen the conversation once rapport is in place, avoiding interrupting or over sharing to ensure the balance of who speaks is in favour of the client

- Show empathy towards the client's situation and feelings

- Watch out for emotional reactions and respond appropriately to enhance trust building

- Be aware of your own emotions – while the focus of the chapter has been paying attention to the client, don't forget that the conversation could trigger your own emotional responses, leaking information to the client

- How to practise using the FORCED and TA Method models

FIVE
Planning Meeting

O nce you have agreed to work with your new client in the initial meeting, put a contract in place and agreed your fee structure, the next step is taking a deeper dive into their current financial situation and their future plans and goals. Part of this stage of the process commonly involves completing a pre-prepared form, known as a 'Fact Find'. You're probably familiar with this type of form, though formats differ. It usually lists the facts and figures of the client's financial position, and obtaining that information is mostly an exercise in going through the form with the client.

The planning meeting not only consists of gathering tangible facts and figures, but also allows the client a chance to verbalise their plans. Discussing future goals can involve a lot of emotion, so you need to be ready to recognise and respond to any signals you see or hear.

In this chapter, we will look at what makes the process of fact finding successful and how a coaching model can help to identify gaps between your clients' goals and their reality. We will also look at the emotions of happiness and fear, how to discuss risk using EI, and finally we will discuss the importance of devising a list of priorities at the end of the meeting.

Fact finding

If you are an experienced financial adviser, you will be confident with this part of the process, however advisers can sometimes get this wrong. You may have noticed this in your own teams or with your colleagues. Here, we will add a few tips and approaches to help you review your processes.

You may feel that the fact-finding process started in the initial meeting, and that is true. Clients may have disclosed information in that meeting relevant to the fact find, but the purpose of the initial meeting is to build trust and strengthen your relationship with your client. Hopefully, now that trust is in place, you can take a deeper dive into the client's current circumstances.

The goal of fact finding is to obtain a thorough record of the client's financial situation. Therefore, you need to re-establish rapport when you meet again. Rapport building and checking should take place at the beginning of every client interaction, so make sure you set time aside at the start of the planning meeting to do this. Don't assume that just because you built a great relationship when you met previously, that the rapport will still be there two weeks later when you have the planning meeting. You need to try to restore that positive state of mind, mutual interest and respect you forged in the initial meeting.

If you feel the client is not disclosing when you start the fact find, take a step back to the rapport building and testing we discussed in the previous chapter. For the client to feel comfortable fully disclosing, they need to trust you, so make sure you have invested the time in laying the groundwork for that.

Questions within the fact-find meeting are a combination of the questions we have already looked at in Chapter 4 (what, where, when, who, how, tell, explain, describe). Closed questions (which are those that can only be answered with a yes/no or a single-word response) should be used to confirm information if the client's answer is vague. Do not assume the answer. Always confirm.

As mentioned earlier, notice that 'why' has been left out of the list of questions. While 'why' is a way of asking an open-ended question, it can be accusatory, and usually the answer to the question involves the person justifying their actions. It is therefore best to avoid 'why' questions as they can lead to the client closing down a little.

If you want to ensure you get accurate information from your client, avoid asking compound questions. This is where two or three questions are asked at once. For example, 'Can you tell me, did you buy your home with a mortgage, and did you use some money from your personal or joint savings to help with that?' Keep your questions as short as possible. It makes it easier for the client to understand and answer you. If you ask compound questions, it is difficult for the client to work out what to answer first. It is also easier for you to hypothesise about what may have triggered any emotion you see or hear if you ask one simple question at a time.

Finally, be careful that your enthusiasm to show the client that you understand them doesn't lead to you finishing their sentences for them. It is easy when you have seen previous clients with similar situations time and time again to think that the answers they will give to certain questions will be the same. However, don't assume you know the answer. It is important for the client to use their own words. Plus, it will damage the relationship and all the hard work you put into building trust in the initial meeting if your client feels they are not being heard.

This stage of the process may also involve a discussion about your client's attitude towards risk, so in this chapter we will look at the role of emotion here.

Goals

The planning meeting can benefit greatly from a coaching approach. You may want to consider the elements of the 'GROW' model of coaching by Sir John Whitmore and colleagues in his book *Coaching for Performance*.[29] For those not familiar with this model, the GROW acronym stands for Goal, Reality, Options and Will. In this context, the 'fact find' captures Reality, which is the client's current financial situation. The Goal stage obtains information about the client's future. It helps the client, and you, to work out if there are any gaps between the client's goals and the reality of their situation, which you can address later.

The discussion about goals and dreams started in the initial meeting with the questions from The Trusted Adviser Method™. You can refer to Chapter 4 to refresh the model in your mind and then implement its elements in the planning meeting to deepen and probe any areas relevant to the client's financial plans.

Is there an ideal mental and emotion state for discussions about the future? If you think back to Chapter 1, emotions have their own motivations. Broadly speaking, it is easier to plan if we are in a positive frame of mind. When we are feeling optimistic, we make plans for the future. If we are in a poor mood (irritable or anxious, for example), we tend to focus on present problems.

Clients have individual differences in how they make goals and see through their actions. The further the future is from the present, the less tangible it is. It is straightforward enough to plan for what you want to do tomorrow, but it is less so if you are planning for a day in ten years' time. There is a greater degree of certainty about the future the closer it is to the present. In behavioural economics, the term is 'delay discounting'.[30] In simple terms, most people would prefer £100 now than £120 in a year's time. But that is the essence of financial planning – giving up money now in return for a future outcome with a degree of uncertainty, such as having enough income in retirement.

Creating financial plans can involve very distant horizons. This can be useful to allow the client to think long term, with ambition, without the practicalities and realities of now. This can, however, also make it hard for some clients to feel the results they hope to achieve are tangible. This varies between individuals. Some people find planning for the long term easy, while others tend towards impulsion and immediate gratification, and find long-term planning difficult. If you find your client is having a hard time making long-term plans, here are some tips:

- Establish clear goals – consider using the SMART formula (Specific, Measurable, Achievable, Realistic, Timebound).

- Visualise plans with charts or cashflow modelling tools – make the goals as tangible as you can.

- Automate – take away the opportunity for impulsive decisions.

- Check in regularly – you might find you need to increase your ongoing contact to keep your client on track.

- Educate – explaining financial principles can help set the context and keep your client motivated.

So far, we have laid the foundations for creating a positive planning environment – trust, listening, communicating clearly and showing empathy. To build on this, you need to highlight successes. If your client has taken positive steps towards their financial future already, bring these to their attention. The emotion of positivity is usually happiness, which we will look at now.

Happiness

© Emotional Intelligence Academy Ltd (2024)

99

Trigger: Pleasure, amusement, relief, excitement.

Purpose: Happiness motivates us to do things that are good for us or to repeat the same or similar behaviours.

Face: Outer muscles of the eye contract, lip corners pulled back, lips can part but not always.

Other nonverbal behaviours: Voice pitch and volume increase with excitement, sighing and relaxed muscle tension with relief, orienting towards the source of enjoyment, elevated posture, leaning in.

Care: The downside of too much happiness is that it can make us overly optimistic and blind to risks. Watch out for genuine versus fake expressions, too. Some people smile just to be polite. We will cover genuine and fake emotions in more detail in Chapter 8.

Responses: Share their enthusiasm. Reinforce and build on positives. Show appreciation. Make sure your matching here is sincere. Remember to consider the refractory period we discussed in Chapter 4.

Risk

Investing and the risks which come with it are part of the financial planning experience. As an adviser, gauging your client's attitude towards risks is part of the process of understanding them so you can make recommendations. The planning meeting is a suitable time to discuss risk. There are many tools available using self-report questionnaires to help clients understand their appetite for risk. While it is not within the scope of this book to review these, we will instead provide an emotionally intelligent way of approaching risk discussions with clients.

As we have said already, emotions often trump logic. They are short-term, quick and dirty responses. You can add value by helping your clients manage their reactions. Here are some tips for achieving this:

- Educate your clients about emotional responses to risks. For example, fear/sadness when markets are falling, or excitement when they are rising. Help your clients understand that these emotions may cloud their judgement in the short term.

- Increase clients' self-awareness by discussing their previous investment experience and emotional triggers around investing. By discussing this with your client, they and you will gain a better understanding of what triggers them. You can build this into your ongoing servicing strategy. If your client is nervous about investing, factor in that they may need to hear from you more often than other clients when markets are volatile. Risk tolerance questionnaires can be discussed here, if you use them, as part of raising self-awareness. You can find versions of these on the web from most financial investment companies.

- Help clients create strategies for managing emotional responses to keep them objective. If you have uncovered triggers, consider what you can put in place to help your client manage them. For example, if your client has previously checked their statements too frequently and volatility has been a trigger for them, agree on times they should check their valuation or suggest that they only review them at your meetings, when they can discuss it with you so they can get your objective input.

- Develop empathy as your first response when your client is emotionally triggered around risks – review the section on communication styles in Chapter 2 on this. As an investment expert, you have an understanding of investing and risk that is often far deeper than your client's, and it can be easy to dismiss a client's initial reactions as irrational or emotional – eg fearful.

This is a good time to explore the next emotion, which is fear.

Fear

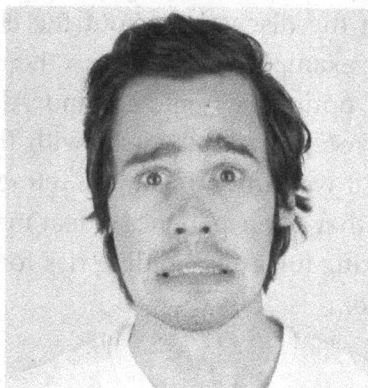

© *Emotional Intelligence Academy Ltd (2024)*

Trigger: Threat of harm to our physical, psychological and/or financial wellbeing.

Purpose: Prepares us to avoid or reduce the threat.

Face: Inner and outer brows up, brows together, eyes wide, mouth stretched.

Other nonverbal behaviours: Freezing, muscle tension, inhalations, retreating (moving away) motions, higher voice pitch.

Care: Fear can turn into anger as we prepare ourselves to deal with the threat.

Response: Hypothesise about the trigger, acknowledge, clarify, educate and reassure.

Remember the refractory period we mentioned in Chapter 4. You will want to be aware if something comes up in the discussion about the client's goals and risk, for example, which causes them to flip out of a positive, optimistic frame of mind. Although you might have recognised and dealt with the emotion, especially if it was around fear, the refractory period might mean that any experience of fear may bias your client's thinking towards avoiding risk for a considerable time after.

Responding to fear

If you notice fear in your client, you can be sure that they may be perceiving a threat of harm – the universal trigger for fear. Threats can be psychological as well as physical, and it is likely to be your client's thoughts around what you are discussing that trigger the emotion when you see/hear it. In your context, perceiving the threat of harm is most likely to be a reaction to actual or potential investment losses, which may threaten a client's livelihood, future goals and security.

The signs of fear may be as subtle as a widening of the eyes. Be aware that if the signs are subtle, the client may not want you to know they are afraid. Therefore, be careful disclosing what you have noticed. It is better to avoid directly acknowledging the emotion or saving the discussion for later when it is safer to do so, and that may be at another meeting.

Here's a worked example of how to respond to fear:

- **Acknowledge** – 'I sense that there might be something making you feel uneasy.'

- **Clarify** – 'Can you share what is worrying you?'

- **Educate** – 'It's natural to be anxious about investment decisions. Let me explain a little more about how this works.'

- **Reassure** – 'I'm here for you throughout this process, if there is anything I can do or explain to help make you feel comfortable, let me know and I'll assist.'

Fear versus anxiety

Now you know more about how to recognise and respond to fear, it is worth discussing how it differs from anxiety.

Fear is an emotion, related to a current threat, which means the duration is seconds at most. Anxiety is a mood that is usually less intense and can persist far longer. It is usually about the prospect of something happening in the future rather than an immediate threat. It can be episodic, or, in more serious cases, it can lead to a more enduring anxiety disorder or phobia which might benefit from professional help.

Work by Jeffrey Gray into fear and anxiety found that different areas of the brain deal with each, making them distinct.[31] Gray found that anti-anxiety drugs do not work on phobias. Consequently, if you are scared of spiders (a fear response), anti-anxiety medication won't help you. Gray is also known for his theory of a behavioural activation system which motivates our behaviours towards rewards, as opposed to a behavioural inhibition system which inhibits behaviour to deal with threats. Gray explained that when these two systems are in conflict, it causes anxiety. In simple terms, if we have a goal we want to attain, but also perceive threats along the way to attaining it, the conflict can cause anxiety.

With clients, this may look like wanting to save for retirement but being inexperienced about investing and worried about potential financial losses. The reward versus threat dilemma can cause anxious feelings. You can support your clients in reducing any anxious feelings they may have about the financial planning process by helping them uncover what they perceive to be the threat. The response pattern to fear is appropriate to use here, too. By helping the client share their concerns you will be demonstrating to them that you understand them, and they will appreciate you being patient enough to help them through any challenges.

There are also individual differences to be aware of here. Some people are quicker to perceive threats than others, and if you recognise that in your client, be prepared to be patient in helping them understand any risks around your advice.

Prioritise

So far in the planning meeting, you have obtained facts and figures about their current financial position, discussed the client's goals and captured their attitude to risk. To finish, you need to agree on a list of priorities with the client. This is the Options and Will sections from the GROW model we looked at earlier.

As you end the meeting discussing priorities, it is an opportunity to pay attention to the client's behaviour to see what may be motivating them. With happiness, some of the behaviours you might see are smiling, head nodding, leaning in and excitement in the voice. These are all signs that what you are discussing is most likely supported by your client.

If your client is using words like 'stability' or 'security', it may signal that different emotional drivers lie behind their decision making. If you notice emotive words as your client is talking about what is important to them, it helps if you repeat them to the client when you summarise your understanding of what they have said. Then finish with a sweep-up question – 'Is there anything else that I need to know that would help me to produce solutions that are going to work for you?'

By the end of the planning meeting, you should have enough information about the client and their financial planning priorities, and about their hopes and fears, to help you deliver your recommendations at the next meeting.

CASE STUDY: Overcoming anxiety

John, a financial adviser with over a decade of experience, met with a new client, Sarah. In her mid-forties, Sarah was concerned about her financial future, especially her retirement savings. The meeting aimed to build a financial plan tailored to Sarah's needs and address her concerns about the future.

During their meeting, John observed Sarah's body language and tone of voice. She seemed tense and avoided eye contact when discussing her current savings and future goals. John used his EI to create a comfortable environment, sensing her anxiety, starting with rapport and actively listening to her concerns without interrupting.

John noticed Sarah's discomfort peaking when discussing market volatility and the uncertainty of future financial markets. Recognising these signs of anxiety, he asked open-ended questions to understand her fears better. Sarah revealed her fear of not having enough savings due to potential economic downturns and unexpected expenses.

John acknowledged her concerns, validated her feelings, and explained the importance of understanding risks in financial planning. He introduced concepts like risk tolerance and risk management, illustrating how different investment strategies can mitigate potential downsides. By breaking down complex financial jargon into relatable terms, John helped Sarah feel more at ease.

John then guided Sarah through an exercise to identify emotional triggers that influenced her financial decisions. They discussed Sarah's past financial experiences, highlighting moments when emotions led her to make impulsive decisions. This reflection helped Sarah recognise patterns and the impact of emotions on her financial behaviour.

To ensure Sarah felt supported, John proposed an ongoing communication strategy. They agreed on regular quarterly meetings and monthly check-ins via phone or email. John emphasised his role as a behavioural coach, not just a financial adviser. This approach reassured Sarah that she has a partner to help manage her emotions and keep her financial plan on track.

By using EI in the planning meeting, John successfully addressed Sarah's anxieties, educated her about the emotional aspects of financial decision-making, and established a supportive, ongoing relationship.

Skill builder

Having read this chapter, consider the following questions:

- How do you currently structure a discussion around goals with your clients?
- What have you learned in this chapter that you can apply to your work?

We are now more than halfway through the book, so it's a good time to take a few moments to reflect on what you have learned so far.

Summary

The planning meeting involves a detailed assessment of the client's financial status and future goals. Effective fact finding not only collects tangible information but also helps clients express their future aspirations, which can be emotionally charged.

Building and maintaining rapport is crucial throughout this process to ensure clients feel comfortable sharing sensitive information. The GROW coaching model will help to align the client's current financial situation with their future objectives.

This chapter has also emphasised the importance of recognising and managing clients' emotions, particularly regarding risk, and we have looked specifically at happiness and fear.

Finally, we explored how the meeting should conclude with a discussion of priorities, using the client's cues and language to identify their motivations and concerns. This comprehensive understanding will inform the recommendations provided in subsequent meetings.

SIX

Implementation Meeting

You have had an initial meeting with your client during which the foundations of a trusted relationship were laid. You took that stage further in your planning meeting by gaining a deep understanding of your client's plans, fears and hopes. Following the planning meeting, you may have had time to research and prepare your advice, and now at the implementation meeting, you need to demonstrate to the client how your recommendations fit their needs. This stage often involves the client making a choice about whether to proceed or not. For some advisers, their fees may be contingent on the client going ahead, so it's a high-stakes interaction for both parties – especially you.

Recommendations

At the beginning of the implementation meeting, as with every meeting, set aside time for rapport building again. Go back to Chapter 2 for information on how to use small talk to begin that rapport, and Chapter 4 to revise the FORCED model to structure your conversations and build on that trust. Doing this will mean that you can gauge where the client is in their thinking when they come to the implementation meeting.

You also need to consider the client's baseline again, as this will show whether buying signals are present and help you gauge your ability to influence them. What can you pick up about the client's mood and behaviours?

Chapter 4 discussed consultative selling, where your sales process is structured around initially gaining an understanding of your client's needs so you can fit your advice and products to them later. Once rapport has been re-established at the beginning of the implementation meeting, you can start by recapping what you did in the planning meeting.

Remember, you are dealing with hearts and minds. The following tips will help you reach into those depths:

- If the client used emotive or descriptive language in the planning meeting, use the same words when you summarise back each goal to the client.

- Recap their priorities, as the client may have reflected on these and changed them since you last met.

- If you have a recording of the planning meeting, you can revisit it before the implementation meeting to see if you pick up on language or behaviours you may have missed before.

Once you have re-confirmed your goals with the client, proceed with presenting your advice. At this stage of the sales process, the balance of who does the talking shifts in the adviser's favour for the first time as technical elements of any products are explained. If recapping goals is *hearts*, then the logical explanation is *minds*. Remember:

- While technical explanations are important to ensure the client understands, don't bore or overload them.

- Technical presentations can link features or benefits to the client's desired outcomes. By doing this, you bring the logical argument into your advice as well as the emotive.

- Consider the client's communication style (see Chapter 2). Do they want lots of detail or are they only interested in the bullet points? You'll have more success and make yourself easier to understand if you communicate using your client's preferred style.

It is important to remember that you want the client to decide whether they will proceed or not at the end of this meeting. At the initial meeting, you specified that the purpose of that meeting was to decide if you would work together, not to agree on fees and products. There is no pressure on the client to make this decision at the end of the planning meeting. Now that you are in the implementation meeting, it is decision time for the client and you will want to carefully make it clear to the client that, at the end of this session, you will need a decision from him/her about whether they will proceed or not.

Cognitive load

Movements of the face aren't always about emotions – sometimes, especially at decision time, the client's face might signal that they are still working things through. Charles Darwin noticed that when people are concentrating or deep in thought, they pose the same facial expression.[32] The facial expressions that show someone is 'thinking hard' (aka 'cognitive load') involve the brows being drawn together and pressed down, and sometimes people may purse or press their lips. Be careful not to mistake this for anger, which we will explore in the next chapter.

This is called Darwin's 'Muscle of Difficulty'. While thinking isn't an emotion, it can convey important information to us, through facial expression and behaviours, that someone may be having trouble understanding what we are saying.

Financial products can be technically challenging, and complaints can often stem from a lack of understanding on the client's behalf. It is therefore the adviser's responsibility to check their understanding, which can influence the client's willingness and ability to proceed. If they are uncertain, they may not be enthusiastic about your advice.

Other behaviours you may notice are changes in body language or face touching, such as the chin hold/stroke.[33] However, if the client touches their face regularly, this may be one of their baseline behaviours and we are only interested if the behaviour is a deviation from baseline. It is also useful to see if there are clusters of behaviour (face + body + voice, for example) as there is no such thing in body language as X = Y, ie one behaviour means one thing. That is a myth, yet so often seen in body language books.

Breathing rate may also change with cognitive load as our brain and major organs demand more resources.[34] Research also shows that we hold our breath when we concentrate, which can be followed by an audible exhalation.[35] These are subtle signs but they may give you a clue as to whether the client is struggling to follow what you are saying. Again, consider what else is going on – is there a *cluster* of behaviours?

Vulnerability

Vulnerability is something we should consider under the banner of ethics. The UK regulator, the Financial Conduct Authority (FCA), defines vulnerability this way:

> 'A vulnerable consumer is someone who,
> due to their personal circumstances,
> is especially susceptible to detriment,
> particularly when a firm is not acting with
> appropriate levels of care.'[36]

The FCA is not messing around here. It is the adviser's responsibility to recognise vulnerability in their clients and take the required action. While there is no prescribed list of personal circumstances provided, we have explained in this book that emotional experience can make us vulnerable. In the test-tube model in Chapter 2, we showed that emotions demand resources, which lowers those left for cognition. Paying attention to emotion and cognitive load is vital at the implementation stage and we have to determine if this is due to our poor communications or whether there are factors affecting the client's ability to assimilate what we are presenting. This could be to do with sensory impairment, neurodiversity factors, or mental/physical conditions including illnesses and disorders, or English not being your client's first language.

A common practice, if any vulnerability is noticed, is to request that an objective third party attend the meetings to support the client – a common practice in the legal system, by the way. It is important to consider who this will be though, and their circumstances. If, for example, your client has recently lost their partner and one of their children agrees to accompany them, even assuming they are 18+, they will have lost their parent, and may equally struggle to give objective third-party support for your client. A third party should ideally be as unaffected as possible by the personal circumstances the client faces – eg a friend.

Responding to vulnerability

What do you do if you notice signs that a client might be vulnerable, and their capacity to make decisions or understand complex information is impaired? There are three ways to consider:

- Defer the meeting until a later time.

- Suggest an objective third party is present.

- Test the client's understanding by obtaining more information about whether they are taking in what you are telling them – ask them to summarise what you have discussed back to you.

Physicist Richard Feynman has been credited with a learning technique which assisted him in understanding complicated topics (although the same technique has also been attributed to Einstein). Feynman realised that to be able to explain something simply requires a deep level of understanding. The method is therefore simple – ask the client to explain it back to you like you're a child.

By asking your client to explain what you have said as if you are a nine-year-old, you are asking them to simplify it. Once you have the response from the client, you can check for any misunderstandings and address any gaps or errors. You can then repeat this until your client is happy, and you are satisfied that they understand. Of course, this must be done in a nonconfrontational way so that the client does not feel patronised or uncomfortable. To prevent this, tell the client that you haven't done your job effectively if they don't understand the information you have given them. Ask them to repeat back to you what you have told them because you need to know that you have done your job well.

If your client still doesn't understand after several attempts to provide additional clarification, you will need to make a judgement on whether proceeding is in their best interests.

More on ethics and dark traits

We like to think of ourselves as good people, yet there are times we can engage in self-deception and put our financial interests above our client's, convincing ourselves that a choice which suits us better will suit the client better too.

In a 2018 study, three groups of advisers were given the task of recommending a choice of two investments.[37] The advisers were given a summary of the client's financial position and details about the two investment options, A and B. In the control group, there were no incentives for either of the investments, and 30.6% of advisers chose A over B. But in the other two groups, it was disclosed that there was an incentive for recommending A over B.

One group was informed about the incentive before making their recommendation and the other after. The group that was informed about the incentive beforehand recommended A over B 61.2% of the time, twice as much as the control group, whereas there was little difference between the group informed about the incentive after they had made their choice and the control group.

The researchers hypothesised that advisers are more likely to fall into self-deception when it is easier to do so, in this case, before they have made their choice. In order to maintain self-image, advisers were less likely to change their advice once they were informed of the incentive, so as to avoid the perception that the incentive had influenced them. However, when the incentive was disclosed beforehand, it clearly influenced advisers' choices, yet they still justified A over B and stated their reasons for their choice.

It is an ethical choice whether you put your client's needs before your own. Being self-aware enough to understand that your own thinking can be influenced by external factors shows a high level of EI.

Research has also shown that advisers who invest in additional professional development and qualifications engage in lower rates of misconduct.[38] One of the aims of this book is to increase your EI skills, which will lead to more empathic advice, thereby reducing misconduct. You can use EI to influence people and help them, or you can use it to manipulate them. If you use it for manipulation, you might get success in the short term, but people will figure out that you have manipulated them and that will tarnish your reputation and their referrals.

The skills and knowledge in this book will give you an edge in your meetings with clients, but being able to read the behaviour of others is a skill which must be managed with care. EI abilities can be used by those who don't have the right intentions towards their clients. The term 'dark personality traits' refers to the combination of psychopathy (lacking empathy), narcissism (grandiose sense of self) and Machiavellianism (using manipulative methods). These are behaviours where individuals tend to put their needs over others.

Lacking empathy, being overly self-promoting, being dismissive of others' emotions or using manipulative tactics to achieve your own goals at the cost of others are all examples of dark trait behaviours. These behaviours can lead to short-term gains but are rarely successful in the long term.

Closing the sale

Once you have explained how your advice and associated financial products meet the client's goals, you need to obtain an agreement to proceed.

Look out for buying signals such as smiling, nodding, being in rapport, maintaining eye contact, leaning in, showing interest, not being distracted and asking questions. If you notice these, it may indicate it is time to ask for an agreement to proceed.

As a rule of thumb, judge the mood of the meeting. If it is positive, then that is a buying sign. If it is not, then you may have to get ready to do more work addressing concerns.

When discussing objections, it is best to adopt an honest and pragmatic approach. As an emotionally intelligent adviser, lead with empathy and see any objections from the client's point of view.

You may encounter that the source of the objection is that the client's emotional reaction is winning over your logical argument. If that is the case, you need to follow the process for responding to emotions found in this book. By acknowledging the emotion, you create space for the client to begin appraising whether their reaction is appropriate and helpful.

For example, if your client wants to save for retirement but has never invested before, their uncertainty may prevent them from taking the steps they need to. By empathising, you avoid dismissing the client's thoughts and feelings. If you get defensive when dealing with objections, your client may sense you have something to be defensive about.

There is a fine line between how far you push with objection handling and conceding that you may not be able to assist further. In the next chapter, we will look at two emotions which will indicate when you have pushed too far.

Leakage

The implementation meeting is a high-stakes interaction for the client, and it may also be for you as the adviser. For some advisers, their fee may be contingent on the client proceeding at the implementation state. If this is the case, there is a chance that you will leak information through your behaviour to your client. It is important to address the fee you are earning from the products you sell upfront so that there is complete transparency with the client.

If your fees are contingent and high, you may feel nervous at this stage and you will need to be careful about communicating this to your client. If the pay-day is particularly big, it may have consequences for you, and you may be already feeling anxious about the client not proceeding.

Remember, one trigger for emotion is others' emotions, and there is an evolved purpose for that. Many years ago, noticing and responding to fear on the faces of others helped alert us to potential threats. Therefore, if a high-stakes meeting is causing you stress, your client may pick up on that and hypothesise about the reason.

If you are worried about any of this, the 'settle the sand' technique we discussed in Chapter 2 can be used to help you prepare for the meeting. Acknowledging and labelling your own emotions can reduce their effect and help you move into appraisal.

The key here is to calm your mind. Nervous feelings are usually the result of the activation of the sympathetic nervous system, which is our fight or flight system. Breathing can be used to calm the nervous system. You can also try the Physiological Sigh.[39] To perform it, inhale deeply, then inhale again for two seconds before slowly exhaling. Repeat two or three times. The relaxed and controlled breathing method is a quick and reliable way of handling anxiety and stress.

Contracting

It's important at the end of the meeting that you explicitly ask for the client to do business with you. Start by observing buying signals such as nodding, leaning forward, asking detailed questions, or expressing agreement with your points. These indicators suggest the client is ready to move forward.

When asking for the business, be direct yet show empathy. Use a statement like, 'Based on our discussion, it seems like [specific product/service] would be a great fit for your needs. How do you feel about moving forward with this plan?' This approach acknowledges their feelings and reinforces the benefits you've discussed.

Once the client agrees, sincerely express your gratitude. 'Thank you for entrusting me with your financial planning needs. I'm excited to work with you.' Gratitude not only signals the endpoint, but it also strengthens your relationship and enhances the client's trust and satisfaction.

Leveraging this positive moment, ask for referrals and testimonials. Explain that their feedback is invaluable: 'Your satisfaction is my top priority. If you know anyone else who could benefit from my services, I'd greatly appreciate a referral. Your endorsement means a lot to me and helps me serve others like you.'

Finally, eliminate any uncertainty by clearly outlining the next steps. Detail the process: 'Next, we'll schedule a follow-up meeting to finalise the paperwork (if needed) and discuss any additional questions you might have. I'll also provide a timeline for implementing your plan.' This clarity helps to build confidence and ensures a smooth transition from prospect to client.

By applying EI throughout this process, you create a positive experience that fosters long-term relationships and potential referrals.

CASE STUDY: Closing a sale

Emily, an experienced financial planner, conducted an implementation meeting with her new client, David. David was initially nervous about the large fees and the significant investment involved. Emily approached the situation calmly and led with empathy. She carefully reviewed the financial plan and explained each recommended product in relation to David's personal financial goals, established in the earlier meetings and re-agreed at the start of the implementation meeting.

When David expressed concerns about the fees, Emily acknowledged his feelings. 'I understand your concerns, David. It's a significant investment, but let's consider the long-term benefits and how this plan will secure your financial future.' She provided clear examples of how her services would pay off in the long run, which helped ease his nerves.

As the conversation progressed, Emily noticed David's engagement and positive signals, such as nodding and asking in-depth questions. Recognising these as buying signals, she confidently asked for the business: 'David, it seems like this plan aligns well with your goals. How do you feel about moving forward?'

David agreed, and Emily expressed her gratitude warmly. 'Thank you for placing your trust in me. I'm excited to help you achieve your financial goals.' Leveraging this positive moment, she asked for a referral: 'If you know anyone else who might benefit from my services, I would greatly appreciate a referral. Your endorsement is invaluable to me.'

Finally, Emily removed any uncertainty by clearly outlining the next steps. She scheduled a follow-up meeting to finalise the paperwork and answer any remaining questions. By using EI throughout the meeting, Emily successfully closed the sale and laid the groundwork for a strong, trust-based relationship with David.

Skill builder

Use the following exercise to check your understanding of contracting a client in your implementation meetings:

- Think of the last client who didn't proceed to work with you.

- Reflect on the reasons why this client did not proceed.

- What additional information have you now learned that you can use in your next implementation meeting?

Summary

The Implementation stage is critical as it is when clients decide whether to proceed, often affecting the financial advisers' fee. Building rapport at the start of this meeting is essential. In this chapter, we explored cognitive load, highlighting signs that indicate whether a client is still processing information. These signs help determine whether the client fully understands the data you have given them. Given the technical complexity of financial products, misunderstandings can lead to complaints, making it your responsibility to ensure client comprehension.

Recognising and acting on client vulnerability means ensuring clients understand the information provided. This is vital, and we have suggested actions you can take if a client's decision-making capacity seems impaired or their level of understanding is not quite where it needs to be.

Finally, we covered identifying buying signals that indicate readiness to proceed and strategies for handling objections.

SEVEN
Difficult Conversations

Financial planning with a client, when done well, can go smoothly and be a huge success. However, sometimes you may hit some 'emotional turbulence' which will draw heavily on your EI abilities.

This chapter explores difficult conversations we, as financial advisers, typically face, and provides tips on how to recognise when things are going wrong, and why. We will cover how you might manage those situations constructively for your client.

Those challenges include:

- Anger and disgust about your advice or your competence

- Irrationality from emotive decision making by the client, eg:

  - Fear and anxiety due to poor performance of a client's investments resulting from economic downturns

  - Manic happiness (or even greed) following news, or an upturn, around one or more of a client's investments

- Sadness due to the client losing a close relative or friend

- Fear due to changes in the health of the client, or someone they care about

- Contempt towards you, or envy/jealousy, due to higher investment performance achieved by others

Then there is the challenge of your emotions. How do you 'manage the chimp' that can easily react destructively towards the client? Equally damaging is suppressing your emotions when your client is rude, offensive, or unjust. Such passivity can erupt later, destroying your client relationship or damaging your wellbeing and confidence.

Let's start with you

You may want to revisit Chapters 1 and 2 to remind yourself of the seven basic emotions, their universal triggers and their unique physiological effects on the body, as these apply to you as much as to your client.

If you can be mindful of your own bodily sensations, you will have mastered the foundation of EI. If not, you will lose yourself in your emotions, react like a chimp, and be so rattled that you will lose your ability to see what's happening for your client. We need to stabilise our own emotional platform before we can see others clearly.

By tuning into our bodily sensations, we can learn to label the emotions we experience. This helps identify the universal trigger so that we can explore what exactly has caused our emotional state – it could be our client's words, their behaviour, our own thoughts, or something else. We can then pause and regulate any emotional reaction that arises if it is detrimental to our wellbeing, or to the interaction we are engaged in. Instead, we can respond appropriately to the context and our goals.

Understanding your emotions

Let's be clear, EI isn't always about suppressing your emotions. Emotions are designed to save our lives, support relationships, and motivate behaviour. If there is a threat of harm towards you or those you care about, then your 'fear' emotion will energise your body to avoid or run away from the threat.

Anger helps you overcome injustices and unfairness by dealing with the threat. If someone threatens your life or those you care about, anger will generate the resources within you to deal with the offender, if and when appropriate – often without thought of the consequences for yourself.

This means that anger can also get you into trouble, if punching an offender is going a little too far. Many of us have probably over- or under-reacted at times and regretted it. Sometimes you might be offended by a client if they are difficult or rude and this leads you to react with anger or to judge them with contempt or disgust. Even if you control your actions, you may not be able to conceal your facial expressions, body language and voice, and the client will pick up these subtle signs. This is because the emotional (limbic system) core of our brain (the one we share with chimpanzees) operates very quickly. The trigger to reaction occurs in less than a second – in fact, things start to happen around the 400-millisecond mark through the amygdala, the root of our emotional brain.[40] The cognitive brain wraps around the emotional brain and is unique to humans and not shared with the chimp. It takes us four to ten times longer (two to five seconds) to think about what is happening to us as a result of the trigger. Therefore, pause, take a breath. Allow your advanced thinking brain to check out what your chimp is planning before it gets you into trouble.

Here, we will look more closely at the final three emotions of anger, disgust and contempt, as these are likely to emerge during the more difficult conversations. Be aware that these signals of emotions can be revealed on your clients' faces... though here we are exploring the fact that you will leak them too.

Anger

© Emotional Intelligence Academy Ltd (2024)

Trigger: Interference with goals (or values).

Purpose: Prepares us to fight and/or deal with interference.

Face: Inner brows down, eyes glaring, tight lower lids, lips rolled in (maybe pressed together also).

Other nonverbal behaviours: Heart rate increase, temperature increase in upper body / face, muscle tension (jaw / arms), voice pitch / volume increase.

Response: Take a breath, pause, hypothesise about the trigger, regulate the emotion if it conflicts with your goals, and choose a constructive response that guides your thoughts and actions.

Disgust

© Emotional Intelligence Academy Ltd (2024)

Trigger: Offensive substance or behaviour.

Purpose: Prepares us to block the offensive substance entering our nose / mouth.

Face: Nose wrinkle and upper lip raised.

Other nonverbal behaviours: Body moves away, guttural stop (yuck effect), gag reflex.

Response: Take a breath, pause, hypothesise about the trigger, regulate the emotion if it conflicts with your goals and choose a constructive response that guides your thoughts and actions.

Contempt

Trigger: Immoral actions.

Purpose: Signals our superiority to others, may prevent a fight.

Face: Unilateral rise of the corner of the lip, or cheek dimpling on one side.

135

Other nonverbal behaviours: Maybe a smug 'Mmmph' sound and head back a little.

Response: Take a breath, pause, hypothesise about the trigger, regulate the emotion if it conflicts with your goals and choose a constructive response that guides your thoughts and actions.

Managing your chimp

These three powerful emotions are often the result of our spontaneous judgement that someone or something is offensive, rude, disgusting or morally offensive. These judgements may be rational and shared by others, but a professional financial adviser knows they are often treading on eggshells when dealing with a client's dreams, life savings, home, family, pensions, and opinions about you and their investment.

This means you need to keep your 'chimp' in its cage unless it's a life or death (for you) situation. This 'chimp' analogy, by the way, was developed by Steve Peters in his book, *The Chimp Paradox* – well worth a read.[41] So, how do we do this?

The following approaches might help you:

1. Stay curious and nonjudgemental about
   your client. If they attack you, get angry,
   or become rude, stay attentive and curious

about what might be going on for them. Treat it as an opportunity to practise and develop your EI. It will stop you from leaking your own fear/disgust/contempt through your face/body/voice.

2. Be attentive. Notice the signals coming from their body/face/voice. Identify the emotion they are most likely feeling and reflect on the universal trigger for that emotion. If you see the signals of fear, you know their wellbeing is being threatened (a 'threat of harm'). Maybe they don't want to look silly due to a lack of knowledge about what you are discussing. Or perhaps it is decision time and they don't feel ready to commit. It could also be about something that has nothing to do with you or what you are discussing. Tread carefully.

3. Be ready to pause. If you sense their emotions or behaviours are triggering your emotions, take a breath... pause... track your sensations and emotions back to the root trigger and choose the best response rather than being a victim of your evolved reactions.

4. Remember that 98% of people are good people. They just seem like assholes every now and again. This is Cliff's mantra, based on an enabling belief that helps him when working in challenging contexts... but not rooted in science (yet)!

5. Also remember, everyone has their own story. We call this 'Story 2', as you may recall from the test-tube model. If you experience inappropriate behaviour from a client (such as them complaining that you don't know what you are talking about) then 'Story 1', the negative story, might be 'They are an idiot and they don't trust my advice.' Story 2, on the other hand, might be that they feel out of their depth and maybe you have presented an investment solution too early. The anger they display could be about them wanting to save face because your knowledge and experience are threatening their ego. You can then check this hypothesis with them and rebuild rapport and trust before you present a solution more in line with their preferences and understanding.

Seek first to understand, and then to be understood

This phrase was coined by Stephen Covey in his book, *The 7 Habits of Highly Effective People*.[12] The first part relies on the FA adopting a curious, empathic and attentive mindset and following the processes laid out in the earlier chapters of this book.

Once you understand your client and their position and goals, you can then support them with a solution they understand and accept. This is tricky, and you may run into conflict and/or emotionally charged situations such as misunderstandings around your role, your advice, or your fees. It is therefore worth exploring the four basic styles of interaction that relate to such situations. Discover your default style using the information that follows, though you are likely to adopt different styles depending on the context, urgency and importance of what is going on, or due to the type of person you are dealing with. That said, you may find that you have a default setting that permeates many contexts.

The main point here is to explore the styles that your client(s) might employ so you can deal with them constructively. These interactional styles are:

- Passive

- Aggressive

- Passive-aggressive

- Assertive

Let's take each in turn.

Passive

Passive interaction is where individuals avoid expressing their opinions or feelings, protecting their rights, or identifying and meeting their needs. They do not respond overtly to hurtful or

anger-inducing situations. Instead, they allow grievances and annoyances to mount, usually unaware of
the buildup. On reaching their high tolerance thresh-
old for unacceptable behaviour, they are prone to
explosive outbursts, which are out of proportion to
the triggering incident. After the outburst, however,
they may feel shame, guilt and confusion, so they
return to being passive.

Passive clients will often:

- Fail to assert themselves when they disagree with
  you, resulting in tacit agreement to your plan but
  then they do not follow through

- Allow others to infringe on their rights
  deliberately or inadvertently; you may have
  crossed the line in your relationship without
  realising it

- Fail to express their feelings, needs or opinions,
  leaving you guessing what they want and
  leading to proposals that aren't accepted

- Tend to speak softly or apologetically so you
  never know what they are thinking

- Exhibit poor eye contact and slumped body
  posture that you may misread as sadness or
  boredom

The impact of this passive communication is that
these clients often feel:

- Anxious because life seems out of their control

- Depressed because they feel stuck and hopeless

- Resentful (but are unaware of it) because their needs are not being met

- Confused because they ignore their own feelings

- Unable to mature because real issues are never addressed

A passive client will say, believe or behave in a way that says:

- 'I'm unable to decide on this right now.'

- 'I need to think about this.'

- 'I don't like conflict.'

- 'Yes, that's ok.'

Encourage your client to get their thoughts and feelings out in the open, but be careful how you respond to passive individuals who seem to be hiding something. They may not be ready to share what's on their mind, or they may not fully trust you yet. When it comes to conflict or emotionally charged situations, get the issue out in the open – whether that's you hiding something or the client. You need to achieve a free, respectful flow of relevant information.

When you pick up signals that rapport is faltering, you may have to test by playing back their words to them or open things up with a few questions or probes. These could include phrases like these:

- 'It might just be me, but I sense that you may have some reservations about my proposals/fees?'

- 'You seem quiet. May I ask what is going through your mind now?'

- 'How do you feel about the process so far?'

- 'You seem to like the proposals, but it feels like you may not be fully on board with everything. What do we need to work on so you can be fully on board with the plan?'

- 'What else do I need to know to make sure the plan is perfect for you?'

Tune 100% into their reply. Then follow their lead, their cues and their reactions.

If they still hold something back and don't seem ready to share it, then you may need to back off and reschedule your meeting. Remember that it might just be about timing, or whatever is going on for them, and nothing to do with you or your proposals.

Aggressive

In this style, clients may express their feelings and opinions and advocate for their needs in a way that violates your rights, or the rights of others. Thus, aggressive clients can be verbally and/or physically abusive.

Aggressive communicators may often:

- Try to dominate you
- Criticise, blame or attack you
- Speak in a loud, demanding and overbearing voice
- Not listen
- Interrupt frequently and finish your sentences

The impact of a pattern of aggressive communication is that these individuals:

- Become alienated from others
- Alienate others
- Generate fear and hatred in others
- Always blame others instead of owning their issues, and thus are unable to mature

The aggressive communicator will say, believe or behave in a way that says:

- 'I'm superior and right, and you're inferior and wrong.'

- 'I'm loud, bossy and pushy – it's got me to where I am today.'

- 'I can dominate and intimidate you because I am wealthier than you.'

- 'I'll get my way no matter what.'

- 'That fee is ridiculous – you aren't worth that amount of remuneration for what you have done.'

At this point, your chimp is yelling 'Story 1' into your ear saying:

- 'You are an ass**le!'

- 'Do they realise how much work I have put into this?'

- 'F**k you!'

Anger from others can easily trigger anger in ourselves, and situations like this can escalate if we are unskilled in dealing with them. While it might feel good to bite back, we may lose our client for doing so. The Emotionally Intelligent adviser, however, will sense the temperature rise in their face, the tension in their fists, and the pressing of their own lips, and realise they must put the chimp in its cage for now, suspend judgements, and get curious. A 'Story 2' can help here. Maybe the client is angry because their ego is dented because they really need your advice. Maybe you have presented a difficult issue to them for a decision and they are just scared. Or perhaps something else is going on at home/work/socially. It's not always about you.

OK... maybe they *are* an ass**le, but caging your chimp, becoming curious, and adopting a Story 2 mindset is better for you... and probably good for them and their investments, too.

Passive-aggressive

With this style, clients appear passive on the surface but act out anger in a subtle, indirect, or behind-the-scenes way. They feel powerless, stuck and resentful – incapable of dealing directly with the object of their resentments. Instead, they express their anger by subtly undermining the object (real or imagined) of their resentments.

Passive–aggressive clients will often:

- Mutter to themselves rather than confront you or the issue

- Use facial expressions that mask how they feel – ie fake smiles when they are angry

- Use sarcasm

- Appear cooperative while purposely doing things to annoy and disrupt

- Use subtle acts of sabotage to 'get even'

The impact of a pattern of passive-aggressive communication is that these clients:

- Become alienated from you or others around them
- Remain stuck in a position of powerlessness
- Discharge resentment while the real issues are never addressed so they can't mature

The passive-aggressive communicator will say, believe or behave in a way that says:

- 'I'm weak and resentful, so I sabotage, frustrate and disrupt.'
- 'I'm powerless to deal with you head-on so I must use guerrilla warfare.'
- 'I will appear cooperative but I'm not.'

People adopting this style may scratch your car with a key for parking in their place rather than discussing it with you openly. They may make you develop, change, redevelop and update your proposals many times only to say they aren't going forward to 'get their own back' on some issue, misunderstanding, or perception that has made them dislike you.

Pause… take a breath… and remember that 98% of people are good people. Get curious about what is going on for them. Turn on your people-reading skills and use some of the probes covered in the 'Passive' and

'Aggressive' sections we explored to get to the real issue. You may end up deciding you and the client can't work together but you will have had a good EI workout!

Assertive

Assertive interactions use a style in which clients (and you) clearly state their opinions and feelings, and firmly advocate for their rights and needs without violating the rights of others. They value themselves, their time, and their emotional, spiritual and physical needs and are strong advocates for themselves while being respectful of the rights of others. Heavenly!

Assertive communicators will:

- State needs and wants clearly, appropriately and respectfully
- Use 'I' statements
- Communicate respect for others
- Listen well without interrupting
- Have good eye contact

The impact of a pattern of assertive interactions is that these individuals:

- Feel connected to others
- Feel in control of their lives

- Can mature because they address issues and problems as they arise
- Create a respectful environment for others to grow and mature

The assertive client or adviser will say, believe or behave in a way that says:

- 'We are equally entitled to express ourselves respectfully to one another.'
- 'I am confident about who I am.'
- 'I realise I have choices in my life, and I consider my options.'
- 'I speak clearly, honestly and to the point.'
- 'I can't control others, but I can control myself.'

Phrases that assertive advisers may use include:

- 'I value you as a client, but when you touch me on the knee, it makes me feel uncomfortable. I need to ask you to avoid this, from now on, please. If so, I am happy to put this behind us and focus on helping you get a great investment plan. Is that ok?'
- 'I know you are disappointed about your investment right now. That is something we discussed at the start. You have seen the long-term performance success of the plans I manage, and I would ask you to consider

staying firm on your plan. We can review your plan every quarter as we agreed and monitor how things are going overall. Is that ok?'

- 'When you tell me I am too expensive it makes me feel uneasy. I have put a lot of work into this investment plan for you, as I know we are dealing with your life savings, and my fees are in line with the fees we discussed at our introductory meeting. I want to do a great job for you, and I want us to agree this is a fair rate. I can stage the initial payment over two months if that helps?'

Which of these four interactive styles of passive, aggressive, passive-aggressive, and assertive resonate with you? If you are generally passive, aggressive or passive-aggressive, you've seen the negative effects that can have on relationships, and you may want to do some work on that. If you are assertive most of the time, then well done. Very few people are. We all fall victim to the other styles, but assertive responses in an EI context, using the skills we've covered in this book, is the way to go, because assertive is more honest. It's more open. The others are too emotive for constructive discussions about serious matters.

Dealing with death and other bad news

In a 1998 study, financial planners who showed higher levels of self-awareness in their EI scores sold more life insurance.[43] Selling life insurance involves discussing difficult topics like accidents, illness or death. Navigating these topics requires high levels of self-awareness which assists the adviser in recognising and managing their own discomfort around these topics.

Mortality or critical illness of the client, or their loved ones, can be tough to discuss, but advisers shouldn't avoid difficult conversations because of their own discomfort. A difficult conversation about death may help the client, and that is the focus of this section.

The issue of death or illness may be raised by the client early in their relationship with you. Sometimes it may take a while before they feel comfortable enough to share at this level with you. Because you can now read people (you may want to review the signs of sadness from Chapter 4), even when the client wants to hide their feelings, you must take care in this area.

Some clients may have rehearsed their death plans and be comfortable discussing them with you, as you are a detached person who can make it easy, even cathartic, for them to bare their souls, fears and thoughts with you. While you may not be a qualified therapist or grief counsellor, you might lean on the EI skills in this book to do what you can when things get sad and difficult. If you care about the person and are willing to give them some of your undivided time, you will do ok. Honestly.

Memories work best for emotional moments and episodes of personal significance, so your support and help for people who are sad will be ingrained in your client's memory and serve your relationship well. Yes… there is a business reason for being kind.

The secret to managing sad moments is to:

- Be 100% attentive
- Create plenty of time for your client – cancel your next meeting if necessary
- Be kind
- Show empathy

Refer to Chapters 1 and 2 for more detail on empathy as it is core to handling high emotions. Even when bad news isn't out on the table, it can serve you well to respond to emotional disclosures, first, with empathy (eg 'That sounds tough!', 'I can see you are really angry!', 'You must be so proud of her!'). Let them vent, share, and open up about how they feel so you can help them process their emotions and segue back into the main purpose of the interaction.

Sorry for my poor apology

Finally… when things go wrong, and it's your fault, then apologise.

Make sure it is a proper apology. Which of these is a proper apology?

1. 'I am so sorry for being late but there was a traffic accident on the motorway/highway.'

2. 'I am so sorry that you feel let down by my advice and services.'

Neither of them. Well done!

Any apology with a 'but' in the middle (like example 1) isn't an apology. The 'but' negates what has come before it.

A more honest response would be:

> 'I chose not to prioritise your meeting over my long breakfast by setting off without allowing for contingencies like traffic accidents, which happen a lot on roads. I have no excuses apart from maybe my own unforeseen serious injury or illness – which didn't happen here. I offer the traffic accident as a weak excuse for my choices (whether it's true or not).'

Harsh, I know, but your client deserves better.

Apologising for how someone feels about your actions isn't an apology either (in example 2). That is making it their fault for being so sensitive. Come on!

Here is an example of a good apology for forgetting to send a document to a client:

'I am so sorry for not sending you the document that I promised I would send to you by last Friday. It won't happen again. I have now created a diary system in which I enter my commitments to you, so this will never happen again.'

CASE STUDY: From aggression to understanding

When his father died, leaving a pension to be split between his three children and four grandchildren, Mr Henshaw contacted the financial advisor handling his father's will. Due to the grandchildren being under eighteen, the FA had to follow guardianship legislation, requiring original ID verification. Additionally, the lack of online forms increased the administrative burden.

Mr Henshaw grew increasingly angry over time. The FA, being naturally passive, struggled with Mr Henshaw's aggressive style and felt bullied. He escalated the issue to his boss, Daniel, who took over the case.

Daniel, assertive by nature, sought to understand the reasons behind Mr Henshaw's anger and build rapport. During one call, he learned that Mr Henshaw was facing financial problems affecting his business, marriage and family life. Receiving the inheritance soon would alleviate these issues.

Understanding this, Daniel respectfully explained the legal obligations they had to follow and why they couldn't bypass the legislation. He assured Mr Henshaw

of his value as a client, promised to expedite the
process where possible, and offered regular updates.
Mr Henshaw appreciated the clear explanation and
chose to stay with Daniel, who successfully managed
his expectations and completed the work to his
satisfaction.

Skill builder

This exercise will help you deal with difficult conversations you may face in the future. Draw on meetings
you have had in the past. Choose three challenging situations (eg a complaint, fee debate, rudeness,
abuse, death, external economic shock, etc) and reflect
on the following questions:

1. What is the scenario?

2. What might the chimp want to do?

3. What could you as the Emotionally Intelligent
   adviser do?

Summary

Effective financial planning can lead to smooth and
successful client interactions, but this may not always
be the case. This chapter has addressed difficult conversations financial advisers might face, giving tips to
recognise when things are going wrong and why. It

provided constructive solutions for managing these scenarios.

Understanding your client's position and goals is crucial for presenting solutions they can accept and comprehend, but this process can sometimes result in emotionally charged situations. To navigate this, we explored the four basic interaction styles: passive, aggressive, passive-aggressive and assertive.

We also delved into the core emotions of anger, disgust and contempt, and discussed their impact on client interactions. Given the sensitive nature of selling life insurance, which involves discussing topics like accidents, illness or death, we provided key strategies for managing these difficult discussions.

By mastering these communication techniques and emotional insights, you can better handle challenging situations, ensuring a more effective and empathetic client relationship.

EIGHT
Ongoing Service Work

Once you have taken your client through the initial, planning and implementation meetings, you may have agreed an ongoing service for which you may be paid a retainer to manage their plan. If that is the case, you will need to agree how many times a year you're going to see them to review the plan. As part of this ongoing service, you will keep track of their financial products from an investment perspective during that time. You will also be proactive about legislation changes. Moreover, there will be an element of delivering customer service.

If you aren't being paid a retainer, you might take a lighter touch. The client might be on your mailing list and get regular updates from you. It's possible that you will pick up the phone every now and then to ask if there is anything you can help them with. For example, if they are moving house, they might need you to help them get a mortgage.

Hopefully, you are proactive in managing your client relationships. You will likely have a client management system in place that enables you to easily set tasks and reminders, and to notify clients of any legislative changes. Technology is picking up pace to assist firms with proactive client relationship management.

We'll demonstrate in this chapter that having a top-notch database of clients that you can segment means you can build EI into your client management strategy easily so that you can continue to communicate effectively, identify emotions and react and manage them appropriately.

Relationship management

Your ongoing relationships with clients are an important opportunity to develop and grow trust by acting with emotional intelligence in how you service your client. After the onboarding stage, you might assume that trust has been earned as the client felt comfortable enough to do business with you. However, trust needs to be maintained and nurtured. If you charge an ongoing service fee, you want to retain your client for as long as you can, and for them to do more business with you in the future and recommend you to friends, family and colleagues as an important source of new clients. In one study into how people found out about their financial adviser, word of mouth accounted for 34% and referrals 24%.[44]

You may remember our definition of trust from Chapter 2 – 'a psychological state comprising the intention to accept vulnerability based upon positive expectations of the intentions or behaviour of another.'[45] Within this book, we have highlighted that inviting your client to be vulnerable in your presence by sharing their hopes, dreams and fears with you, and reciprocating when appropriate, builds trust. In the definition above, the client is also vulnerable because they are relying on your professional expertise. If you have delivered on their priorities in the implementation meeting, you will have begun to earn their trust.

We might assume that trust continues to grow with relationship duration, and research supports this, but the correlation is small.[46] There are other moderating factors which influence ongoing trust in a relationship. Earlier, we used the metaphor of a trust account. Trust needs to be maintained, and the actions of you and your firm can either credit or debit the balance.

However, if duration isn't the main method that trust continues to develop in a professional relationship, there are other factors we need to pay attention to. To repeat a mantra in this book, when we pay attention to and are careful with the emotions of others, trust grows. When we are neglectful of others' emotions, trust withers. So, we need to pay continued attention to the client's emotional as well as financial needs in our professional relationship.

Delivering value

If a client engages the services of an adviser, they have placed themselves in a vulnerable position. They have trusted you as their adviser and they consequently expect value from the relationship. If you arrange investments for your client, they might equate the value you bring to the returns they may achieve. But you are not responsible for the market, so attributing investment returns to you is an error.

If it's not investment returns, then the value you bring to the client might not be obvious. Vanguard research suggested that 1–2% per annum can be obtained through 'behavioural coaching'. They attribute this to helping clients navigate emotions during the investment journey, so they stay on track and act objectively rather than emotionally.[47]

It's hard to put a value on the influence you can have keeping your clients on track, rather than allowing them to act emotionally and potentially against their best interests. What is reassurance worth? A few objective words at the right time can make all the difference in the client's long-term investment returns.

The monetary benefits, such as tax planning or investment returns, are available to the DIY investor who does their own research. While it may be tempting to use these to show your client the value of using your service, they may realise that they could have achieved the same results themselves – for far less in fees.

In a study from 2009, advisers who responded to a survey stated they spent 25% of their time helping with a range of nonfinancial issues with their clients, acting as coach/counsellor on such things as life goals, health issues, career advice, bereavement, family conflict, divorce and legal problems.[48]

It can be hard, if not impossible, to quantify the value of these non-financial benefits, but by using the skills and knowledge within this book to recognise and respond to emotions appropriately when these issues arise, they will be perceived as valuable in your clients' eyes.

Remember, your clients disclose intricate details about their lives, and once they trust you with that information, they may feel comfortable talking to you on a regular basis about non-financial topics. You can hold a safe confidential space for clients to discuss things which may be on their minds which they have not discussed with anyone else. Friends are often not the best listeners. They want to give their opinion or advice rather than simply being a sounding board. Often people don't want to disclose their balance sheet to others. Do we have that level of disclosure with our friends, or even our families? You may have experienced the situation as an FA where the wife of a client leaves the room and her husband tells you that he has another £300K stashed elsewhere that his wife doesn't know about.

Of the advisers in the 2009 study, 57% had been told a secret and were the only person the client had disclosed it to. Creating an environment where clients can do this is highly valuable, yet difficult to quantify in monetary terms.

Intermittent rewards

When we receive something unexpected that is of value to us, we feel good. The reason is due to the release of a chemical called dopamine in the brain. Dopamine has many functions, but here we are interested in how it works in relation to providing an amazing client experience.

Research by Wolfram Schultz suggested that there is a learning phase where dopamine is released in response to a new stimulus. However, once the learning phase has passed, dopamine levels reduce.[49] That tells us that unexpected rewards are more exciting than predictable rewards.

This is important for client servicing as things like sending birthday cards or festive gifts to clients often seem like a sensible strategy. But as festive occasions and birthdays happen each year, the effect of gifts for these events becomes less significant over time... unless your client has come to expect them and then suddenly doesn't receive them.

Research into the brain's reward centre suggests we are far more tuned into novelty and unexpected rewards. This sounds like it might be difficult to integrate into your client servicing strategy, but it's easier than you think.

During the onboarding state, you recorded clients' preferences, hobbies, likes and dislikes. If you have this data recorded in a client management system or similar, you can use it to create an annual plan for sending 'I saw this and thought of you' gifts. These need to be highly personalised and distributed randomly to have the maximum impact.

An example might be buying a book on cycling for a new client who mentioned they have recently taken it up as a hobby. Or buying theatre tickets for a show a client mentioned they have been wanting to see.

In Schultz and Romo's work, they set up an experiment where monkeys had to learn which box their food was in.[50] There were two lights – red and green. When the red light came on, the food was in the right box. When the green came on it was in the left one. But the pattern was random, and soon the monkeys associated the light with rewards and became excited when the light went on, not when they opened the box and saw the food.

Be the light for your clients, integrate intermittent rewards into your service strategy and they will remember how you made them feel.

One word of warning though. If you are dealing business to business, you need to ensure that gifts are not seen as inducements.

Personalised communication strategies

If you have paid attention to how the client communicates in various media (face-to-face, email, phone, etc), you may have picked their preferred style. Is this a person who wants bullet points, or do they need a lot of detail? Do they prefer visual representations to written explanations?

Aside from considering any communication preferences for those who may have visual, auditory or other neurological impairments, capturing and using individual styles can help your clients understand you and engage with your ongoing service.

A good starting point is asking clients what their preferred styles for communication are, rather than assuming. For some clients, instead of creating a written investment summary, you could:

- Create an infographic

- Use charts, graphs or slides

- Record a short video of you talking about the report

Consider the tone and adjust accordingly as some clients may expect a more formal tone than others.

When writing emails:

- Use clear headlines to make them easier for your client to understand

- Use bullet points to get important information across

- Highlight important action items if you need the client to do something

Ongoing communication is an area where obtaining feedback from your client is key. Ask your client periodically if you are getting it right. There is a sweet spot for communication. Too little leaves the client worried, but too much may overdo it. Each client will vary in terms of what they need.

In earlier chapters, we advised that you may need to increase the amount of communication around key events like market movements or legislative changes with some clients. Other clients may need reminders about the long-term benefits of the work you are doing together to help them stay on track.

As you implement your ongoing service and communication strategy, you may spot signs of upcoming issues you need to address, which we will look at next. First, we will cap off our series of emotional faces with the 'social smile'.

The social smile

In Chapter 5, we looked at the pleasurable emotion, happiness. Have a look at the two photos here. Which one is a genuine smile, and which one is fake?

© Emotional Intelligence Academy Ltd (2024)

With the genuine expression, the difference is in the eyes. In a genuine happy smile, the muscles around the eye contract, creating noticeable wrinkles in the outer corners of the eyes. Be careful though, as some people have wrinkles here that may become more pronounced when smiling. There is also a difference in the eye cover fold below the eyebrow. It covers more of the upper portion of the eye, which is another indicator that the emotion accompanies the expression.

What is the 'fake smile' for? Termed a social smile, its purpose is to communicate several different things such as politeness or to mask our emotions, or to 'grin and bear it'.

We need to pay attention to this difference because it shows that the client may not be feeling the emotion they are conveying and, considering the context and their words, that may be relevant or not. Or they may be masking an emotion they don't want to disclose. Paying attention to subtle signs like this is important if you want to keep relationships on track.

Keeping relationships on track

Alongside the social smile, watch out for signs of contempt from your client, as this is important for proactive relationship management. The aim is to spot problems before the client has vocalised them so that we can get them out in the open and attempt to resolve them. This will help maintain and grow relationships.

John Gottman identified contempt as one of the 'four horsemen', which are attitudes or behaviours that we need to watch out for because of their potential for causing destruction in relationships.[51] The four are:

- Contempt, showing a lack of respect
- Criticising, complaining or attacking that can be personal
- Defensiveness, self-protective responses
- Stonewalling, being unresponsive

If you notice the social smile, contempt, or any of these behaviours, you may need to acknowledge that there might be something wrong that the client hasn't disclosed. Responding with, 'I get the sense that there may be a problem here that needs addressing', gives the client the opportunity to open up. If they don't vocalise what is troubling them, you might follow up by explaining that you value your working relationship and are happy to address any concerns the client has. If they still don't respond, they may not want to discuss the issue with you, or you might not be the issue and something else may be on their mind. If you follow the process of acknowledging, clarifying, responding and reassuring, you can hopefully address any issues early and proactively before they grow into problems that later may be more difficult to overcome.

Research suggests that there is an emotional cost of withholding complaints.[52] A person who with-holds complaints may ruminate, playing thoughts of what is troubling them over and over again in their head. This can lead to emotional exhaustion and passive-aggressive behaviours which we looked at in the last chapter. By helping your client voice their grievances, you help remove the weight of the prob-lems, and that is positive for your relationship.

Client referrals and testimonials

At the beginning of this chapter, we saw how impor-tant client recommendations are as a source of new clients. Testimonials about the work you have done for your clients are another valuable source of new business. Showcasing your work transforms financial planning from a potentially intangible service, allow-ing future clients to see the value you bring through the words of others you have helped. Think about those non-financial benefits mentioned earlier, such as reassurance and support with life planning. If those are captured in testimonials they may resonate with potential new clients.

Is there a good time to ask for referrals and testimoni-als? Yes – when you spot the signs of positive emotion.

At the end of the implementation meeting, or as part of your ongoing service, you may have an opportunity to channel the client's appreciation and positivity into a recommendation or a review.

Pay attention to the mood of the meeting. If you spot smiling, enthusiasm and positivity, take the opportunity to ask for a referral or testimonial. For example, you might start this conversation by saying, 'I can see you are pleased with the work we have done for you and we'd love it if you could share your experience with friends or colleagues; would you be open to writing/recording a testimonial for us?'

By capturing the right moment, you can increase your referral and testimonial rates. This is such a huge source of new clients that you can't leave it to chance. Take control and put in place a process to ask whenever you spot that the time is right.

It can be confrontational, so you've got to handle it right. Ask 'Are you really happy? So, would you recommend us? Do you have anyone in mind who would benefit from this?' When they mention their contact's name, say, 'Would you mind if I approached them?' By doing this, you now have a prospect. And if they make the contact first, your timing could be perfect. Really, you have nothing to lose. This is an opportunity cost but if you don't ask, it means the loss of a new client.

Skill builder

It's now time to reflect on what you have learned in this book.

Review the twelve abilities which make up the EmotionIntell model of emotional intelligence. Where do you think your strengths and weaknesses are?

Self-awareness:

- Perceive and label your own emotions as they occur.

- Identify and anticipate triggers for your own emotions.

- Appraise the appropriateness of initial emotional reactions to goals.

Self-management:

- Interrupt your initial thoughts and reactions.

- Adopt strategies to manage your own emotions when appropriate.

- Initiate and regulate your emotions to support goals.

Social awareness:

- Read others' communication signals across multiple channels.

- Hypothesise about others' emotions.

- Appraise options for your own actions relative to goals.

Social interaction:

- Engage others in a way that is appropriate to the goals of the interaction.

- Interact appropriately to analyse and understand others.

- Influence others towards goals.

Finally, if you didn't get a chance to do the self-assessments at the beginning, here's the link again: www.eiagroup.com/HeartOfFinance.

CASE STUDY: David and Julie

David and Julie started using a financial planner to help them manage their investments with the goal of retiring early in ten years' time, at age 48. During the initial discussion and planning meetings, David and Julie explained that they sometimes have differences of opinion regarding risk. Julie is more comfortable with risk taking in life, and David is cautious and worries about negative outcomes.

Over the last year, their FA met with them every six months to review their plan. During those meetings, a mixture of written updates and visual representations were presented to consider the differences between how David and Julie take in information. During the year, markets fell 20% at one point and the FA contacted David immediately to reassure him of their decision to invest long term to achieve their goals and remind him of their discussion that volatility may happen. David explained he had been worried and had felt uneasy that morning before the phone call. He was pleased that the reassurance from the adviser landed at the right time.

Julie asked the FA if she should invest in 'meme stocks' after reading an article about the returns others had achieved. Her FA helped her understand that her excitement was blinding her to the risks, and that 'meme stocks' were not an ideal solution to help with their plan. He delicately introduced a more rational view so as not to 'burst her bubble'.

David and Julie celebrated their tenth wedding anniversary in September. They went back to the hotel in the Maldives where they spent their honeymoon. Their FA contacted the hotel and arranged for a private dinner on the beach one evening as a surprise. David and Julie couldn't believe it, and they contacted him on their return to say how thankful they were for the thoughtful gesture.

The year wasn't without challenges, as during one of the meetings Julie was unhappy with their investment performance following the fall in the market. She was quieter than usual during the review meeting, which was a change in baseline. The FA asked if Julie had something she wished to discuss, but Julie said she was fine. Julie's social smile, however, indicated that

she was masking an emotion. The adviser suggested
that any issues are best dealt with out in the open
and that the meeting was a safe space to discuss
any problems or concerns. Julie explained she had
a different understanding of how the investments
should have performed. The adviser empathised with
Julie's concerns and asked her to explain further. It was
clear that a misunderstanding had occurred between
Julie and the FA, and once he explained further
how the investments worked, Julie was happy her
misunderstanding had been dealt with.

Summary

After the initial, planning and implementation meetings, ongoing service may involve a retainer for
regular plan reviews and proactive management,
including legislative updates and customer service.
Without a retainer, interactions may be more sporadic,
with occasional calls or emails.

In this chapter, we discussed how to use EI to maintain client trust and ways to deliver value to your
clients by providing non-financial support and offering personalised communication. We learned how
unexpected rewards, such as personalised gifts, can
enhance client relationships.

Monitoring client communication styles and adjust-
ing accordingly is crucial for effective ongoing service.

Recognising genuine versus social smiles helps identify potential issues early.

Finally, we discussed the importance of getting client referrals and testimonials, which are vital for new business and how having a proactive strategy can significantly enhance your business growth.

Conclusion

When you started this book, we gave you the chance to complete a free self-assessment of your own emotional intelligence. Here is the link again in case you haven't yet done it: www.eiagroup.com/HeartOfFinance.

If you have already completed it, we'd suggest you go back to that assessment result again and review it now that you have read this book. If you wish, you can also take an in-depth assessment – the *e-Factor* – that objectively tests your EI and gives you an EQ score out of 200. You can access the *e-Factor* here: www.eiagroup.com/tool/e-factor. We are confident your score will be enhanced by what you have covered in this book.

The results of the *e-Factor* assessment may highlight chapters that you might want to go back and reread. So, keep this book handy so you can refer back to areas where you scored low so that you can refresh those skills again in your mind.

We also advise that you build your learning into your Personal Development Plan (PDP) to harness those skills you want to improve and implement in your daily interactions with your clients. Think about where you want to be in three years' time, for example. Then consider what is the first thing that you can tangibly implement now. If it's building rapport, practise it and see what results you get. Just take one or two things that you can implement now and once you get feedback about how that's working, move forward from there.

Once you've done your PDP, that's where we can help you. You can contact us for support to help you integrate these tools and concepts into your work by attending one of our training sessions online. Or you might want to sign up for our next live event. We can create bespoke training for your team's needs.

Go to www.eiagroup.com/course/emotional-wealth -the-financial-planners-guide-to-ei-mastery or www. raiseyourei.co.uk to find out more about our online courses, our live events and to contact us for bespoke training for your team.

Notes

1 Luskin, F, Aberman, R and DeLorenzo, A, *The Training of Emotional Competence in Financial Advisers* (Consortium for research on Emotional Intelligence in organisations, 2015), www.eiconsortium.org/reports/emotional_competence_training_financial_advisors.html, accessed 1 July 2024

2 Lansley, C, 'Emotionintell: A generic emotional intelligence model', doctoral thesis (PhD), Manchester Metropolitan University in collaboration with Emotional Intelligence Academy (2020), https://e-space.mmu.ac.uk/627419, accessed 9 July 2024

3 Ekman, P, 'What scientists who study emotion agree about', *Perspectives on Psychological Science*, 11/1 (2016), 31–34, www.paulekman.com/wp-content/uploads/2013/07/What-Scientists-Who-Study-Emotion-Agree-About.pdf, accessed 9 July 2024

4 LeDoux, J, *The Emotional Brain: The mysterious underpinnings of emotional life* (Simon & Schuster, 1996)

5 Vitelli, R, 'Can you change your personality?', *Psychology Today* (7 September 2015), www.psychologytoday.com/gb/blog/media-spotlight/201509/can-you-change-your-personality, accessed 9 July 2024

6   Lansley, C, 'Emotionintell: A generic emotional intelligence
    model', doctoral thesis (PhD), Manchester Metropolitan
    University in collaboration with Emotional Intelligence
    Academy (2020), https://e-space.mmu.ac.uk/627419,
    accessed 9 July 2024. See also: Lansley, C, 'What scientists
    who study emotional intelligence agree on' (Emotional
    Intelligence Academy, 2021), www.eiagroup.com/wp-
    content/uploads/2023/06/What-EI-scientists-agree-on-.
    pdf, accessed 9 July 2024
7   Grabenstetter, S, 'The value of emotional intelligence in
    financial planning relationships' (eMoney, 2021), https://
    emoneyadvisor.com/blog/the-value-of-emotional-
    intelligence-in-financial-planning-relationships, accessed
    9 July 2024
8   Ortolani, A, 'Emotional needs outweigh financial for people
    working with FAs' (planadvisor, 2023), www.planadviser.
    com/emotional-needs-outweigh-financial-people-working-
    financial-advisers, accessed 9 July 2024. See also:
    - www.sjp.co.uk/academy/events-and-
       insights/news/harnessing-emotional
       -intelligence-why-women-make-great-advisers
    - www.fa-mag.com/news/-emotional-intelligence-
       -called-key-to-unlocking-advisers-potential-73203.html
    - www.scribd.com/document/89214457/
       Ameriprise-Financial-Adviser-Study
9   R Hunt, 'Seventy-one percent of employers say they value
    emotional intelligence over IQ, according to CareerBuilder
    survey' (press release) (CareerBuilder, 2011), https://press.
    careerbuilder.com/2011-08-18-Seventy-One-Percent-of-
    Employers-Say-They-Value-Emotional-Intelligence-Over-
    IQ-According-to-CareerBuilder-Survey, accessed 9 July
    2024
10 Van Rooy, DL and Viswesvaran, C, 'Emotional intelligence:
    A meta-analytic investigation of predictive validity and
    nomological net', *Journal of Vocational Behavior*, 65 (2004),
    71–95
11 Luskin, F, Aberman, R and DeLorenzo, A, *The Training of
    Emotional Competence in Financial Advisers* (Consortium for
    research on Emotional Intelligence in organisations, 2015),
    www.eiconsortium.org/reports/emotional_competence_
    training_financial_advisors.html, accessed 1 July 2024

12 Goleman, D, 'An EI-based theory of performance'. In: D
     Goleman and C Cherniss (eds), *The Emotionally Intelligent
     Workplace* (Wiley, 2001)

13 Enhelder, M, 'Emotional intelligence and its
     relationship to financial advisor sales performance'
     (Proquest, 2011), www.proquest.com/openview/
     df60692890a832a4bd2b908731747336/1.pdf?pq-
     origsite=gscholar&cbl=18750; McCarthy, A, 'Exploring
     the relationship between financial adviser emotional
     intelligence and perceived client relationship
     markers' (Proquest, 2020), www.proquest.com/ope
     nview/12e40871381722af4771542e206b6567/1?pq-
     origsite=gscholar&cbl=44156; Woodfall, J, 'A correlational
     study: What relationship exists between emotional
     intelligence and job performance in self-employed financial
     advisers?' (Manchester Metropolitan University, 2020)

14 Goleman, D, 'An EI-based theory of performance'. In: D
     Goleman and C Cherniss (eds), *The Emotionally Intelligent
     Workplace* (Wiley, 2001)

15 Epstein, S, 'What does it mean to hold space?', *Psychology
     Today* (25 May 2023), www.psychologytoday.com/gb/
     blog/between-the-generations/202305/what-does-it-mean-
     to-hold-space, accessed 9 July 2024

16 The Emotional Intelligence Academy, 'Communication
     assessment tool', www.eiagroup.com/tool/
     communication-style-assessment-tool/, accessed 9 July
     2024

17 Ekman, P, *Emotions Revealed: Recognizing faces and feelings
     to improve communication and emotional life* (Times Books/
     Henry Holt and Co, 2003)

18 LeDoux, J, *The Emotional Brain* (W&N, 1999)

19 McClue, B, 'An introduction to behavioural finance',
     Investopedia (2024), www.investopedia.com/
     articles/02/112502.asp, accessed 9 July 2024

20 LeDoux, J, *The Emotional Brain: The mysterious underpinnings
     of emotional life* (Simon & Schuster, 1996)

21 Danziger, S, Levav, J and Avnaim-Pesso, L, 'Extraneous
     factors in judicial decisions', *Proceedings of the National
     Academy of Sciences*, 108/17 (2011), 6889–6892

22 Rousseau, DM, Sitkin, SB, Burt, RS and Camerer, C, 'Not so
     different after all: A cross-discipline view of trust', *Academy
     of Management Review*, 23/3 (1998), 393–4042

23 Aron, A, Melinat, E, Aron, E, Vallone, RD and Bator, RJ, 'The experimental generation of interpersonal closeness: A procedure and some preliminary findings', *Personality and Social Psychology Bulletin*, 23/3 (1997), 363–377

24 Schneeberger, T, Reinwarth, AL, Wensky, R, Anglet, MS, Gebhard, P and Wessler, J, 'Fast friends: Generating interpersonal closeness between humans and socially interactive agents', *Proceedings of the 23rd ACM international conference on intelligent virtual agents*, 15 (2023), 1–8

25 The Emotional Intelligence Academy, 'SCANS™ – Six Channel Analysis System', www.eiagroup.com/white-paper/scans-six-channel-analysis-system, accessed 9 July 2024

26 Lansley, CA, Garner, AJ, Archer, DE, et al, 'Observe, Target, Engage, Respond (Oter©)' (Emotional Intelligence Academy, 2017), https://e-space.mmu.ac.uk/620124/1/EIA-CNAB-SRI-iALERT-White-Paper-restricted-Apr2017.pdf, accessed 9 July 2024

27 Aron, A, Melinat, E, Aron, E, Vallone, RD and Bator, RJ, 'The experimental generation of interpersonal closeness: A procedure and some preliminary findings', *Personality and Social Psychology Bulletin*, 23/3 (1997), 363–377

28 Ibid

29 Whitmore, J, *Coaching for Performance: The principles and practice of coaching and leadership* (Nicholas Brealey Publishing, 1992)

30 Hirsh, J, Guindon, A, Morisano, D, et al, 'Positive mood effects on delay discounting', *Emotion*, 10/5 (2010), 717–721

31 Gray, JA and McNaughton, N, *The Neuropsychology of Anxiety: An enquiry into the functions of the septo-hippocampal system* (2nd ed) (Oxford University Press, 2000)

32 Darwin, C, *The Expression of the Emotions in Man and Animals* (D Appleton and Company, 1898)

33 Mueller, SM, Martin, S and Grunwald, M, 'Self-touch: Contact durations and point of touch of spontaneous facial self-touches differ depending on cognitive and emotional load', *PLoS One*, 14/3 (2019)

34 Grassman, M, Vlemincx, E, Von Leupoldt, A, et al 'Respiratory changes in response to cognitive load: A systematic review', *Neural Plasticity* (June 2016)

35 Alpher, VS, Nelson, RB and Blanton RL, 'Effects of cognitive and psychomotor tasks on breath-holding span', *Journal of Applied Psychology*, 61/3 (1986), 1149–1152

36 FCA, 'Finalised guidance FG21/1: Guidance for firms on the fair treatment of vulnerable customers' (Financial Conduct Authority, 2021), www.fca.org.uk/publication/finalised-guidance/fg21-1.pdf, accessed 9 July 2024

37 Gneezy, U, Saccardo, S, Serra-Garcia, M, et al, 'Bribing the self', *Games and Economic Behaviour*, 120 (2018), 311–324

38 Kowaleski, Z, Sutherland, A and Vetter, F, 'Can ethics be taught? Evidence from securities exams and adviser misconduct', *Journal of Financial Economics*, 130 (2019), 159–175

39 Ashhad, S, Kam, K, Del Negro, CA, et al, 'Breathing rhythm and pattern and their influence on emotion', *Annual Review of Neuroscience*, 8/4 (2022), 223–247

40 Guex, R, Méndez-Bértolo, C, Moratti, S, et al, 'Temporal dynamics of amygdala response to emotion- and action-relevance', *Scientific Reports*, 10/1 (2020), 11138

41 Peters, S, *The Chimp Paradox* (Vermilion, 2012)

42 Covey, S, *The 7 Habits of Highly Effective People* (Simon & Schuster, 2001)

43 Goleman, D, 'An EI-based theory of performance'. In: D Goleman and C Cherniss (eds), *The Emotionally Intelligent Workplace* (Wiley, 2001)

44 Pattison, K, 'What are the key drivers in client acquisition?', *IFA Magazine* (4 June 2021), https://ifamagazine.com/what-are-the-key-drivers-in-client-acquisition, accessed 9 July 2024

45 Rousseau, DM, Sitkin, SB, Burt, RS, et al, 'Not so different after all: A cross-discipline view of trust', *Academy of Management Review*, 23/3 (1998), 393–4042

46 Vanneste, BS, Puranam, P and Kretschmer, T, 'Trust over time in exchange relationships: Meta-analysis and theory', *Strategic Management Journal*, 35/12 (2014), 1891–1902

47 Kinniry Jr, FM, Jaconetti, CM, DiJoseph, MA, et al, *Putting a Value on Your Value: Quantifying vanguard adviser's alpha* (The Vanguard Group, 2019)

48 Sussman, L and Dubofsky, D, 'The changing role of the financial planner part 2: Prescriptions for coaching and life planning', *Journal of Financial Planning*, 22/9 (2009), 50–52

49 Schultz, W, 'Predictive reward signal of dopamine neurons', *Journal of Neurophysiology*, 80 (1998), 1–27

50 Schultz, W and Romo, R, 'Dopamine neurons of the monkey midbrain: Contingencies of responses to stimuli

eliciting immediate behavioral reactions', *Journal of Neurophysiology*, 63 (1990), 607–624

51 Gottman, JM, 'A theory of marital dissolution and stability', *Journal of Family Psychology*, 7 (1993), 57–75

52 Liu, E and Roloff, ME, 'Exhausting Silence: Emotional costs of withholding complaints', *Negotiation and Conflict Management Research*, 8 (2015), 25–40

Appendix: The Trusted Adviser Method Questionnaire

The Trusted Adviser Method (TA Method™) uses a framework of open questions combined with financial themes and words for eliciting **fears**, **goals**, **satisfaction** and **preferences**. You can construct your own questions, this questionnaire provides a set of fifty-four questions we have created for you.

Each question below contains a keyword that relates to one of four aims of the questions. These areas and the keywords are:

- For exploring **fears**: concerned / worry / anxious / risk / secure / safe

- For understanding **goals**: aspire / dream / goal / envision / hope / wish / plan / aim

- For gauging **satisfaction**: satisfied / content / happy / frustrated / disappointed / pleased

- For discussing **preferences**: prefer / like / comfortable / inclined / interested / value

Set 1: Establishing basics

1. **Retirement:** How **satisfied** are you with your current retirement plan?

2. **Investing:** What do you **like** most about your current investment approach?

3. **Family:** Who in your family do you **prefer** to discuss your financial plans with, and why?

4. **Home:** What do you **value** most about your current living situation?

5. **Education:** How **pleased** are you with your education funding strategy?

6. **Tax Planning:** How **satisfied** are you with managing your taxes?

7. **Business:** If you own a business, what do you **value** most about it?

8. **Work:** What aspects of your work are you most **interested** in?

9. **Career:** How **content** are you with the financial trajectory of your career?

10. **Lifestyle:** What lifestyle **comforts** are most important to you financially?

11. **Spending:** How **satisfied** are you with your current spending habits?

12. **Debt:** How **comfortable** are you with your current levels of debt?

13. **Friends:** Who among your friends do you **value** discussing financial decisions with?

14. **Hobbies:** What hobbies **interest** you?

15. **Health:** How **satisfied** are you with your financial planning for health-related reasons?

16. **Fitness:** What aspects of your fitness lifestyle are you most **pleased** with regarding financial commitment?

17. **Spirituality:** How do your spiritual beliefs influence your financial decisions in a way that **pleases** you?

18. **Giving and charity:** What aspects of your charitable giving **interest** you most?

Set 2: Exploring financial behaviours and attitudes

1. **Retirement:** What **concerns** do you have about your retirement plans?

2. **Investing:** Describe how you feel about the **risks** involved with your current investments.

3. **Family:** How important is it for you to **secure** a financial future for your family?

4. **Home:** What changes would you like to make to align your living situation with your financial **goals?**

5. **Education:** What are your **aspirations** for your or your family's educational future?

6. **Tax planning:** What **frustrates** you about your current tax planning?

7. **Business:** Explain how you handle financial **concerns** in your business?

8. **Work:** How **secure** do you feel regarding financial stability in your current job?

9. **Career:** Describe what you **like** about your work.

10. **Lifestyle:** How do you **prefer** to balance financial decisions and desired lifestyle changes?

11. **Spending:** What spending pattern changes are you **interested** in making?

12. **Debt:** What strategies are you **interested** in exploring to reduce your debt?

13. **Friends:** How do your financial discussions with friends influence your financial **plans?**

14. **Hobbies:** Describe how you **aim** to balance your budget to accommodate your hobbies.

15. **Health:** What **concerns** do you have about funding future health needs?

16. **Fitness:** How do you **plan** to support your fitness goals in the long term, financially?

17. **Spirituality:** Describe how your financial practices reflect your spiritual **values.**

18. **Giving and charity:** What **goals** do you have for your philanthropic efforts?

Set 3: Deepening understanding of values and future planning

1. **Retirement:** What **worries** you most about your financial security in retirement?

2. **Investing:** What long-term financial **aspirations** are you aiming to achieve through your investments?

3. **Family:** What legacy do you **hope** to leave for your family?

4. **Home:** What are your long-term financial **dreams** for your home?

5. **Education:** What **concerns** do you have about financing education in the future?

6. **Tax Planning:** What are your long-term **plans** for optimising your tax situation?

7. **Business:** What financial **risks** keep you up at night as a business owner?

8. **Work:** How does your current job **security** impact your financial planning?

9. **Career:** What are your ultimate career **goals,** and how do they integrate with your financial planning?

10. **Lifestyle:** What financial **fears** do you have regarding your future lifestyle?

11. **Spending:** What financial **plans** do you have for your future lifestyle?

12. **Debt:** Describe your **concerns** about managing and eliminating debt.

13. **Friends:** How do you **envision** your financial interactions with friends impacting your future?

14. **Hobbies:** What **plans** do you have for the funding of your hobbies in the future?

15. **Health:** How **anxious** are you about the potential financial impact of health issues?

16. **Fitness:** What are your long-term **goals** for maintaining fitness, and how do they relate to your financial planning?

17. **Spirituality:** How do you **hope** your spiritual beliefs will guide your financial decisions?

18. **Giving and charity:** What **worries** you about your ability to continue supporting charitable causes financially?

Acknowledgements

The authors would like to thank Siobhan Costello for her help in planning the book and turning our ideas into reality, the team at Rethink Press for making the editing and publishing process seamless, and the whole team at EIA Group for their input and providing permission to use some of the models and images in this book.

In addition, we would like to thank Dr David Matsumoto and Frederick Kermisch for their input and advice during the final draft stages of the book production. We also owe thanks to our communities and clients for advice on the book cover and title.

The Authors

James Woodfall

James is a highly experienced financial planner, having previously run his own financial planning business, which he exited in 2022. While studying for his Masters, James researched the relationship between emotional intelligence and job performance in financial planners. He now works with financial services firms consulting on how they can use emotional intelligence to improve individual and company performance.

🌐 www.raiseyourei.co.uk

in www.linkedin.com/in/james-woodfall-raise-your-ei

Cliff Lansley

Cliff is an expert in emotional intelligence (EI) and behaviour analysis. He has worked with clients across the globe and in many sectors – including the military, intelligence, law enforcement and business – helping them to read, understand and influence others when it matters. He is one of the world's best human truth/lie detectors and is engaged by WarnerBrothersDiscovery as scientific adviser and presenter on criminal behaviour analysis for their real-crime series *Faking It: Tears of a crime*. As an entrepreneur who has owned, led and sold businesses, he understands the principles of asset and wealth management, and he uses his research and expertise to help financial planners, their businesses and their clients succeed. He is a Director of the Emotional Intelligence Academy, and provides live, virtual and online training and coaching services and products up to MSc level.

🌐 www.eiagroup.com

in www.linkedin.com/in/clifflansley